Potter's Child

10 Habits to Shape and Mold Outstanding Children

STEPHANIE MATHEWS

Potter's Child

10 Habits to Shape and Mold Outstanding Children

Stephanie Mathews

2022© by Stephanie Mathews

All rights reserved. Published 2022.

BIBLE SCRIPTURES

Author's photo courtesy of The Teal Album Photography (thetealalbum.com)

Other photos by Paul Knudsen Photography

Printed in the United States of America

Spirit Media

www.spiritmedia.us

Spirit Media, and our logos are trademarks of Spirit Media

1249 Kildaire Farm Rd STE 112

Cary, NC 27511

1 (888) 800-3744

Self-Help, Motivational

Paperback ISBN: 978-1-958304-34-1

Hardback ISBN: 978-1-958304-33-4

Audiobook ISBN: 978-1-958304-18-1

eBook ISBN: 978-1-958304-17-4

Library of Congress Control Number: 2022921294

SPIRIT MEDIA

Register This New

Book

Benefits of Registering*

- FREE replacements of lost or damaged books
- FREE audiobook—Get to the Point by Kevin White
- FREE information about new titles and other freebies

www.spiritmedia.us/register

*See our website for requirements and limitations

REVIEWS

Bethany Academy
(ICSE/ISC Residential/Day School & Junior College)

Vennikulam, Thiruvalla, Kerala 689 544,
Ph: 0469 3205319/2650578(Office)
Website: www.bethanyacademy.com
E-mail: bethanyacademy@gmail.com

Office of the Patron

Review: Potter's Child by Stephanie Mathews

"The best investment you can make is to first teach yourself lessons you never learned."- Potter's Child by Stephanie Mathews

Isn't it just amazing when you come across one of those books that gets your undivided attention, encourages you to reflect on life's journey and fills you with peace knowing that you are not alone on this beautiful journey? Stephanie's Potter's Child is one of those books for me.

Stephanie has sprinkled throughout the book personal anecdotes *(which is my favorite kind to read)*, applicable life stories, plenty of real-life examples, practical advice and Biblical encouragement throughout each chapter.

Her language is simple. Her artwork is refreshing. Her thoughts are profound yet easy to grasp with the finesse of a talented and genuine author.

Throughout the pages of Potter's Child, Stephanie Mathews makes sure that with each page her readers will walk away with practical ways to nurture oneself and one's loved ones.

Mary Sheba Mathews

Senior Principal

Bethany Academy, India

Every child is precious and deserves very special care

5

This book is well balanced, highlighting the necessary habits needed to be instilled in our children (Prov 22v6). These habits are being eroded in most families today, thereby placing Stephanie Mathews' work on a very important pedestal. I pray that whoever reads this book will not be too philosophical but digest the intended simplicity of formulating good habits in our children.

Betty Mareesa
Preschool Director
Zimbabwe, Africa

When I was sent the first draft chapter to read, the first few lines itself made me say "wow" as the words spoke straight to the heart. It was poetical, with personal testimonies, and the author's own transparent experiences all bringing out the enchantment, practicality and the reality of prayer. What a different approach to prayer I thought. Then I read the second chapter and realized the book was offering more. I requested the whole draft and saw what an immense and valuable resource it is for parents and for everyone for the matter of personal growth and maturity and to train up a child in the right Godly way right from the start. This is one book everyone will say after reading I wish I had this when I was just starting up. Surely divine wisdom was operating in the author. May the Lord be glorified and the readers be edified through this remarkable book.

Rev. Arnold Rajan
Pastor, City Tabernacle KL, Malaysia
Principal, Logos Academy

I have read the book *Potter's Child* by Stephanie Mathews. It's a very nice book which will help many parents raise their children. If we can apply at least five or six of these habits when raising our child or children, they will be wonderful human beings.

Yovani Nullathumby
Mother of a 4 yr old girl
Saint Pierre, Mauritius

This book resonated with me so much as I live life with building habits on a daily basis. I highly recommend this book to teens, parents, and regular people who sometimes struggle with building habits in many different aspects of life. This book is raw that shares the snippets of people's lives and that helps resonate with so many, be it kids or adults and from different walks of life. This book is not a one-time read but instead it's a life changing book that everyone should have a copy of on their night table and read a chapter often to remind themselves of building good habits.

Dharshini Munesinghe
Mother of a teenager
Austin, Texas USA

Stephanie touches on how we develop habits from what we experience in our lives and that we need God (faith) to help us understand those experiences and how to make them result in positive outcomes. As the reader we can take away those habits to develop in our children. The Potter's Child is a refreshing way of narrating various life stories including the author's personal life stories to explain how each of those developed habits can be passed down to create an overall positive change in a child's behavior.

Honestly, I've been married for 30 years and have an 18-year-old son, but it is not too late to start a couple of these habits myself.

Elizabeth Thomas (Sunu)
Mother of a teenager
Dallas, Texas USA

My favorite chapter is 7! All I can say is, this is an extraordinary book!

Joneil Joseph
Dad of a 2 year old boy
Brunei Darusallam
A well done and beautiful read!

Potter's Child reflects aspects and principles of nurturing by experiences and through the author's autobiography. It's always a good read when life lessons are reflected by experiences rather than rules. This warm and lighthearted literature grounds any reader as we emerge from surviving an unnatural, protracted period of isolation, separated from loved ones and routines that helped us thrive.

Dr. Bawani Marsden
Fellow of the Royal Australian and New Zealand College of Psychiatrists (RANZCP)
Bachelor of Medicine, Bachelor of Surgery (MBBS)

Thank you for sharing this marvelous book!

They say a parent's life doesn't come with a manual, but this book is as close as it gets… spiritually, emotionally, and in the most joyful way to get by one's day! So many golden nuggets of wisdom and deep insight afterthought in upbringing … Well done!

Marina Simon
Singapore

Stephanie is a phenomenal writer. What a wonderful book. I am confident it will be a blessing to many!

Binu Samuel
Author of Quest for More:
A One Year Devotional Through the Bible

It was an honor and pleasure to read your book! I know how much this means to you and now your wisdom, knowledge, personal experiences and your beautiful heart will be shared with the world. I pray your words of wisdom will help others see the importance of being present in our lives and teaching those around us to love well. Reminding ourselves not to let the comparison traps trip us up. We are God's creation, not that of man and walking the road that is less traveled is so much more rewarding. Congratulations & can't wait to see how God uses you & your book for His glory.

Debi Alston
Gigi (grandma) of three

I love, love, love this book! It was such a joy to read. Stephanie touched on all of the seemingly forgotten rules of child raising that were once the standard! It is all the words of wisdom that I would have liked to have given my daughters when my grandchildren were born. They would have accepted them in the form of a book. I am quite sure that this book will be very successful!

Linda Dunlop (Volunteer)
Children's Advocacy Center
of Rockwall County. Texas, USA

An extremely powerful story of a mother from her experience in habit learning and mastering as she grows through its discovery. This debut is astute about the stories told, decorated with the ability to tune information at just the right clip: a hint here, a shading of meaning there, a beautifully paced buildup of what-ifs followed by an inevitable reversal of readerly forecasts or, in some cases - even through an exhilarating and bewildering pull of the entire narrative rug. All of these are mind-opening strengths in discovery and growth painted into "Potter's Child". Make your bed (Get the job done!) on 88 was definitely a favourite. Such a piece written with much relatability and truth truly sang the words my own mother would say to me on days she felt I really needed to hear them. The themes expressed outline instances that parallel your everyday routine with a better version of it, and mirroring as such - from what is, to what could be - is wholly absorbing as it is a bird taking its first flight and soon finding its home in the clouds. It's change waiting to happen, in the best way.

Shridevi Jeevan Simon
Author of Silk
Kuala Lumpur, Malaysia

Potter's Child captures a narrative every mother would want her child to know, from starting their day in making their beds to ending their days kneeling in prayer before one. As a mother myself, I can say truly from the very bottom of my heart, that every ideal this book holds is an ideal I would encourage my own children to represent themselves with - spiritual bliss and faithful grace when you surrender yourself to God.

Uma Revathy
Mother of four young adults
Kuala Lumpur, Malaysia

Dedication

<><><><><><><><><><><><><><><><><><><><><><><><><><><><><><><><><><><><><><><><><><>

Mom, thank you for instilling valuable life skills in me through your role as a mother; I can now pass them on to my children and share them with the rest of the world. I love you more than you know and will forever be grateful.

Sophia and Jude, my darling twins, I pray you will be both blessed and a blessing to those who surround you. Always remember whose child you are. You are a Potter's Child. You are mummy's/mama's precious miracles, and I love you both with all my heart.

Acknowledgements

〰〰〰〰〰〰〰〰〰〰〰〰〰〰〰〰〰〰〰〰〰〰〰〰〰〰〰〰〰

The team who worked with me to complete *Potter's Child* are special people in my journey who made it possible to turn thoughts, ideas and research into valuable personal development material. I am grateful and honored to have such talents who were willing to contribute their precious time to impact the readers of Potter's Child. The resources and stories from generous contributors allowed me to put together this book to best serve you. From the brain dump process, through journeying with a writing coach, meeting virtually with the publisher and working with the editorial team, it took weeks and months for completion. It truly takes a village to raise children and a great team to get something worthy created. If you read a little of each person who crossed paths with me and became part of my journey, you will be amazed how God works. This team allowed me to execute my work and establish my dreams.

Acknowledgements

The team who worked with me to complete *Potter's Child* are special people in my journey who made it possible to turn thoughts, ideas and research into valuable personal development material. I am grateful and honored to have such talents who were willing to contribute their precious time to impact the readers of Potter's Child. The resources and stories from generous contributors allowed me to put together this book to best serve you. From the brain dump process, through journeying with a writing coach, meeting virtually with the publisher and working with the editorial team, it took weeks and months for completion. It truly takes a village to raise children and a great team to get something worthy created. If you read a little of each person who crossed paths with me and became part of my journey, you will be amazed how God works. This team allowed me to execute my work and establish my dreams.

"Teamwork Makes The Dream Work."

Here are the powerhouses who molded this book to existence alongside with me:

I cannot thank Barbara Hemphill enough. We met at an event months before this book came to fruition. I was close to making a u-turn to go home because it looked as if a storm was approaching and I had many thoughts racing in my head about work and my children. "I am sure nobody will mind my absence" I thought. Then again, it was not polite to RSVP and not show up especially for a friend who was willing to give me advice freely when I first ventured into small business, I kept talking to myself. Somehow, my good habits made way for me to take one closer step to achieving my dreams. Mathew Thomas prophesied in his speech that day at his event, he said "This room is filled with visionaries…….. your life is about to change." Barbara took me under her wings for months, patiently reading my brain dumps and guiding me to completion. Oh! What a journey of life changing events. "Dress up and show up", I have heard that many times, on that day it proved that showing up matters whether you are excited to attend or not.

When I talked to Kevin White of Spirit Media, I knew right away that he was going to publish my book. This book is for His glory and Kevin's vision aligns with mine. We are just clay in the Potter's Hands. I want God to take over and "steal my show" and Kevin believed the same. With his team: Carlene Byron, Marj, Carol and Jay, I am able to hold a book I can be proud of... for his glory! God made a way, just like he always does, and I am grateful and thankful for this team.

Thank you dear Professors from UTD: Professors who guided me to share my ideas where it would flourish to become a reality. Professor Bryan Chambers who believed in me and gave me the green light to present my elevator pitch for the Start-Up Launch Project. Professor Robert Wright who gave me an opportunity to be part of his StartUp Launch Program. When Professor Wright told me to read "Goodnight Story for Rebel Girls" and asked me to turn to the blank pages at the back of that book to write my story, he led me to think bigger than what I had in mind. The stories of women who created history broadened my vision and possibilities. Teachers are significant people in our lives and I was blessed to be his mentee.

I am extremely grateful to Jessica! Jessica Arriaga who contributed the research work for this book. She is not an ordinary friend; she is a special individual whom I have worked with since college. I have a beautiful mural on the wall of my event space in Rockwall, Texas that Jessica painted. I value her love and friendship. She is the kind of friend who would go the extra mile for a friend even literally; she drove me to the hospital during a medical emergency. I was able to deliver my twins safely because she was willing to drive back all the way for me although she was close to forty-five minutes away from where I lived. I am honored to have worked alongside her for this book. She is currently preparing to be a pediatrician, and she will truly be a blessing wherever she goes. She is outstanding in many ways. She is an example of a Potter's Child.

I must thank Kalpana Paranjothy for her creative illustrations. Kalpana was probably twelve or younger when I first met her at The Temple of Fine Arts, a renowned dance and music academy in Kuala Lumpur, Malaysia. Kalpana walks, talks and breathes art. She is an art teacher who also completed her master's in music in Ireland. I was thrilled to work together with her to discuss the illustrations. Life is full circle, the little girl I used to exchange smiles within the hallway before dance classes is now a team member for my meaningful project. Thank you, Kalpana!

I am indebted to Susan Ann Samuel who contributed her beautiful poetry at the beginning of each chapter. She is an author from India who wrote "Unseen Yet Seen", a story about her dad's journey as a missionary. She is currently a PhD student in England. When I first approached Susan years ago about working together, she was quick to respond with a "Yes!" I was thrilled when I received an answer as I am her avid fan. I know for sure that her poems alone will impact readers, and my message comes through exquisitely through her poems. Her wisdom and in-depth understanding of my content is a blessing.

Special thanks to Binu Samuel who is a dear friend and one of the authors of a devotional, "Quest for More." She is also a writer for the Proverbs 31 ministry. Her testimony in the first chapter is a beautiful story about how God uses His children to bless each other. Her husband blessed a man with shoes, but we in return are blessed by this testimony, as believers who often hear people doubt the power of prayer. I am so thankful for this story - and I know reading it will impact someone. I also mentioned two teenage boys who were loading the dishwasher in Chapter 3, those well raised boys are her sons. I have a lot to learn from Binu and her husband Sunil about parenting.

I would also like to thank Physician-Scientist Dr. Sanya Thomas, whom I fondly call Sanya. She is a relative from India and we have shared many meaningful life events together, I am so proud of her accomplishments as she pursues her dreams in America. She was willing to be our "overqualified nanny" during her transition periods caring for our premature twins during the most difficult first few months. Dr. Thomas helped Sophia and Jude several times when they choked after feeding (a gagging condition premature babies suffer from due to acid reflux) which left me panicking. I appreciate her taking the time to contribute despite her busy schedule as a Physician-Scientist (Boston Children's Hospital/Harvard Medical School).

I am also grateful for Jane Rowland, my Pastor's wife from Trinity Church Dallas. Jane and her family prayed fervently for me to have a baby for years. When my Pastor came to the hospital to pray for my daughter Sophia who was admitted to the NICU (Neonatal Intensive Care Unit), he told me that Jane insisted that he visit Sophia. My baby girl was discharged from the hospital the very next day, indeed there's power in prayer; power in Jane's prayers!

I very much appreciate Me Ra Koh who allowed me to share her powerful message about suicide in Chapter 1. When I first heard Me Ra's story at a women's networking event, I was bawling, I walked up to buy her book. I loved her transparency and courage to share what most people avoid bringing up. Me Ra's story will heal many broken hearts and for that I am thankful for her willingness to help my readers. Her books about photography and her recent book "4 Minutes to Hear God's Voice" are powerful; packed with nourishment for the soul.

I would also like to express gratitude to Dr. Elizabeth R. Thomas, a dear friend whom I met through mutual friends. Some people leave lasting impressions in our hearts and Dr. Thomas whom we fondly call Betsy is one of them. Her willingness to help, love for Jesus and humility is what draws me to her. I had the privilege to attend Bible classes and read the beautiful devotional "Quest for More" which she co authored and I am thankful for her contribution as a pediatrician and mom for this book. Her contributions will be a blessing for families who struggle to make time to pray.

Thank you Dr. Paul for the invaluable contribution. Jesus Calls Ministry played a big role in my life. I started listening to Dhinakaran's messages when I was nine years old. We had cassettes of the songs playing at home and Jesus Calls magazine I've read. I have been to the life changing rallies held in Malaysia by Brother Paul Dhinakaran years later even after his dad passed away. I read the devotionals online to-date, these messages were my guiding lights and source of peace during my trying times as a young adult. It was a blessing to personally meet Brother Paul, his wife Sister Evangeline and their children here in Dallas. Dr. Paul's generous contribution for Chapter One: The Power of Prayer is God's way of showing me how he works beyond what we imagine or can ask for. I also want to thank Praveen Rajkumar who made this possible as he helped me gather this contribution.

I am grateful to my husband Dr. John Mathews who gives me the wings to soar. I am able to dream big because I am married to someone who works hard to make dreams a reality. I wouldn't have been able to complete this book without John's help in many different areas, including watching our toddlers while I have my peace and quiet time to complete this book. My twins and I are blessed to have a husband and dad who supports and loves us. I don't usually address him as Dr. Mathews, but in this book I wanted to because he truly earned it. I married a medical student who started residency, I have seen him toil through his journey: praying, working hard for many years, continuously learning and always dreaming big. But what sets him apart is his love for his patients; I am honored to be his wife.

Thank you for the support and countless lessons I have learned throughout life dear family, friends near and far, teachers, bosses, pastors, and acquaintances (a big part of this book). I will forever be grateful to the contributors who weren't directly involved. Both positive and negative life lessons were applied. I am also grateful to all those who allowed me to experience bad habits; unknowingly giving me examples which I could use. I read a funny sign once which said, "You have the right to remain silent around me, anything you say can be used in my next book." This quote brought a wide smile to my face when I first read it, it is quite true.

Last but not least, without God's hand on the wheel, none of my efforts would produce a worthy product shaped and molded for His Glory. I praise and thank God for his soft promptings, wisdom, guidance, the right people, love and endless opportunities to complete this book; a project that he planted in my heart. He gave me the credentials as a mother to write and publish this book; in his time. I am humbled to be called a Potter's Child. Thank you Jesus!

Contributors:

Susan Ann Samuel

 https://www.linkedin.com/in/susan-ann-samuel-7734961b1/?originalSubdomain=uk0-0-0

Dr. Paul Dhinakaran

 https://www.jesuscallsministries.org/dr-paul-dhinakaran/

Me Ra Koh

 https://fioria.us/

Binu Samuel

 https://whispersandfringes.com/about-us/

Dr. Elizabeth Thomas

 https://whispersandfringes.com/about-us/

Dr. Sanya Thomas
 https://www.linkedin.com/in/sanyathomas/

Jane Rowland
https://trinitydallas.com/about/

Barbara Hemphill
https://barbarahemphill.com/

Kevin White
https://www.linkedin.com/in/kevinwhiteus/

Jessica Arriaga
https://www.linkedin.com/in/jessica-s-arriaga-pina/

Dr. Elizabeth Thomas
https://www.linkedin.com/in/drelizabeththomas/

Sharon Patricia D'Cruz
https://www.linkedin.com/in/sharon-d-cruz-79441bb9/?originalSubdomain=au

Foreword from Barbara Hemphill

◇◇◇

I love how God puts people together for His glory! That is certainly the case with my first meeting with Stephanie. We met at an event neither of us was excited to attend but felt we should. Within minutes of conversation, we knew God had arranged it. The book you are holding is the reason! I'm so excited you are reading it. I pray you will share it whenever and wherever possible because these lessons our children desperately need to learn.

Table of Contents

Introduction:
Habits and How They Help Us

<><><><><><><><><><><><><><><><><><><><><><><><><><><><><><><><>

Who wants to think of habits? If a practice is a good one, it hardly ever crosses your mind. You benefit from it every day. Maybe you have a good habit of brushing your teeth twice a day or playing outdoors with your kids to get fun exercise, and you don't even notice. Maybe your good habits include pausing before responding when someone's words have made you angry or resentful.

If a habit is bad, we might see how it causes problems and be overwhelmed by how much work it would be to change. Those could include practices like, "If it's chocolate, I'll take two!" or hours-long screen scrolls, ignoring everyone in our natural world.

Good habits represent the world where we come from and whose Children we are. You've heard the saying, "The apple doesn't fall far from the tree." For our children to have the opportunity to imitate good habits, we have to develop good habits for them to emulate.

Instead of giving children what we never had, it's better to model and teach life lessons to help them in their daily lives. Every lesson we have learned is valuable to someone who never did. With all this in mind, I want to share *Potter's Child* with the world. My experiences may be a source of inspiration or lessons, or maybe just a gentle nudge and a reminder to help drop a bad habit and pick up a good one. But either way, children are surrounded by their families, peers, and a village of people modeling potential behaviors for them.

Every person has good and bad habits. When we were young, we were sponges who imitated and followed our siblings or parents' footsteps. As we grew older, we realized we had picked up some bad habits along the way. *Potter's Child* reminds you that it's never too late to know and do better. You can be ten or sixty-five; this book will serve you in some way to understand how good habits can make a difference.

We are molded and shaped by our parents and our environments. Those around them incredibly easily influence some people. Being "cool" or "mean" is a habit some learn that can be dropped. It's never "cool" to bully a child or an adult with words or actions. I was appalled to discover a book that taught people how to insult others. Why would someone write that? Bullying and insults have caused young people to end their lives to escape the pain. People practicing healthy relationship habits like kindness, generosity, and encouragement will help prevent suicides, suicidal thoughts, and other mental health problems.

We are the Potter's Child, the clay, and when we allow God to be our guiding Parent, he will mold and shape us to be the best versions of ourselves – the people God designed us to be. We can surrender to Him at any age and hand over all our bad habits to pick up new ones. But please understand: You don't have to be a Christian to read this book. It is a tool that can add value to anyone's life.

A few life experiences led me to create something of value to help kids and adults (myself included) build good habits. Creating something of value was also an idea from God when I prayed. In 2017, while studying business at college, I designed a board game to help teach good life habits and presented it in a "Mini Shark Tank" event to seven Dallas investors. One of the "sharks" challenged my credentials, and he wasn't the first. "What do you know about kids?" he asked, as others have along the way. "You don't have children!"

> **When we allow God to be our guiding Parent,**
>
> **He will mold and shape us to be the best versions of ourselves**
>
> –
>
> **the people God designed us to be.**

In the mini shark tank, I gave an answer that silenced everyone in the room. I pointed out that my entrepreneurship professor had been lecturing about businesses for years, although he didn't own one. You don't always need direct experience when there are many other ways to learn.

I kept hearing that challenge over the years, though. And since my miracle babies were born and I became a twin mom, I keep discovering that no matter how much I know about children, there's so much more to learn, despite my real-world experience. Parents all learn as we go. Our children teach us lessons we might not have cared to pay attention to when we were kids. Plus, every child is different.

Still, there are some basics we all need – every Child and every adult—Manners matter in every part of the world. Our behavior toward other people judges us. In many countries, children and parents focus on accolades and degrees. Those are important, indeed. I believe that education is our passport to a comfortable and secure life. But comfort and beauty have little value when they rest on a rotting foundation. What will become of that beauty and comfort if the foundation collapses?

In various books and research studies, happiness and success are always defined in many ways. They don't mean the same thing to everybody, although not everyone realizes that.

Success to you might be graduating from the most prestigious school or it might be living a comfortable and happy life with family and friends who enrich it. It doesn't matter how we perceive success and happiness, though. What matters is how our habits make or break us and nurture or destroy our relationships.

A mouth full of rotten teeth will not give you the best smile. In the same way, a person who has the habit of making silly jokes or gossiping can be their worst enemy because people will get offended and begin to avoid them. Without discipline, we cannot achieve good grades or attain our goals in sports or almost anything we pursue. Building relationships and intentionally improving ourselves are essential for our emotional, spiritual and physical well-being.

Why is Potter's Child so important? This book reminds us that although we live in a world that focuses on beauty and appearances, exterior appearances don't last. Beauty fades, and over the years, people will forget that you once were the quarterback of your high school team. So there's no fame in your game. As you get older, people recognize instead your heart that is willing to serve and the people whose lives you have added value to. It doesn't matter what you have gathered and collected. What matters most is who you are.

Habits are the Foundation of Our Lives

When I handled an extensive home remodeling project, nearly every visit exposed new damage that needed to fix. The process wasn't unlike how people experienced us: our image, personality, and character. An inexperienced observer of homes will see a beautiful beachfront house with appealing light fixtures, paint color, furnishings, and decorations. They will say, "Oh wow! It's gorgeous!" But what that inexperienced eye sees and what I have seen are different. The seemingly beautiful house had not received the care it needed. It wasn't too late to repair it, but it required a lot of work! The wood was rotting beneath each window panel, the electrical wiring was rusty at the connections, the plumbing tended to clog, and the oven smelled of fish. The casual observer fails to see the underlying issues that undermine the home.

Doesn't that sound like our relationships? Everything in life requires us to go back to the "foundation." An excellent sturdy foundation in a home, association, or personality provides the base for something valuable. And just as we have to maintain our homes and possessions consistently, we need to work constantly on the foundational habits that form our relationships and personality, learning, growing, and allowing God to mold and shape us through books, life lessons, and experiences.

One of the best ways to learn is from someone else's experience. People hurrying to grow up don't realize that every phase is essential and will come in handy at some future date. They find themselves later looking for resources to help them learn what they tried to skip. *Potter's Child* is written to help you and the children you love build character. The contents are poured out from my heart, life experiences, generous contributors and with the help of God to remind us that overlooked fundamentals make a crumbling foundation.

I remember when my cousin struggled to grasp certain subjects in medical school. My husband, who had completed his medical degree, kept reminding her to "Go back to basics! Go back to basics!" So, likewise, this book focuses on the basics of an extraordinary life! Our children and our well-lived days are the most important products we can give the world. So, I pray you will be blessed as you read and share this book.

Books played a significant role in my life as I was growing up. Books are a way I've learned from other people's experiences, even when I haven't known anyone I can learn from directly. Books taught me, informed me, and transformed me. They became companions when I was alone working in different parts of the world. They gave me insights into the authors' experiences and allowed me to travel to places I had never been. Books have widened my knowledge and expanded my desire to continue learning. They can renew and refresh my thoughts when I am down and confused. What I have learned from books has allowed me to view circumstances and life positively.

My favorite book is the Bible. Unlike other books, it's my compass to navigate life. My late aunt presented me with a Bible in which she wrote a beautiful message that included these words: "Many books will inform, but the Bible will transform you. Life without Christ is a hopeless end. Life with Christ is an endless hope. Make Pam [my family nickname] a blessing, Lord, make her a blessing to someone today, tomorrow, and every day." Her messages are embedded in my heart, and I pray the same for you. I pray this book will bless you today, tomorrow, and every day.

Potter's Child is a product of my faith, my beliefs, and the lessons I have learned from my family, friends, peers, bosses, and people I have been surrounded by. I struggle with certain habits, but I constantly remind myself of the value that mastering good habits will add to my life. It's a journey, and I invite you to join me to master good practices together.

Special Thanks

It has been a blessing to me to share and work alongside Barbara Hemphill. Her rich experiences in helping people to form habits that benefit everyone every day have helped develop me and continue to shape my growth. Through the years, this book was on the back burner, and Barbara urged me forward. She fanned the flame of my restless spirit in a way that amazes me. God was setting a stage and illuminating it with the best lighting. I'm grateful for the ray of hope that Barbara is in my life and for our God, who continues to surprise me.

Chapter 1

The Power of Prayer

Softly you knock, unsure with an unuttered cry,
and the doors shall open,

Just as you are you fall into the arms of Love and
your lips give way to amen,

Love will find you there, Love will rise up for you,
pursue powerfully for you!

This is no more your story, so step aside dear
friend, mercy is going to break through!

Let the rain water the Earth, let the harvest begin,

Let the fields of gold greet the gaze of the Sun in

Perfect harmony! Let the power of prayer pave
your way,

Potter's child, forlorn in the mist of sorrow, let
Love make you stay

In the power of Love! Let Love shape you today
and every other day.

You're the clay, and you're being skilled and
blessed, each time you pray.

Susan Ann Samuel

The Habit that Fuels a Lifetime

Faith is the gift of having a relationship with God. A person of faith finds themselves praying in every circumstance. The habit of relying on God in prayer is the only thing that won't change in a child's life but will expand and strengthen them when they grow older.

It's a habit to ask God for help before reaching out to anyone else. Believing in the power of prayer is a habit. The help we can receive from people around us is not going to be the kind of help that comes from God. In many circumstances, God will use his children to provide for our needs, but in some circumstances, God comes through directly. We won't always be able to hover around and protect our children the way we want to, but we can cover them with our prayers. No weapon is stronger than prayer. Our enemies can plan and scheme to destroy our lives, but prayer is more powerful than any of their agendas. We just have to believe!

I have picked a few stories about answered prayer for this chapter to give you hope and encouragement. The best gifts you can give your child are those of faith and the habit of prayer. There's power in it when you

> *The best gifts you can give your child are those of faith and the habit of prayer.*

kneel, close your eyes and reach out to God, the creator who made you for a purpose. God has shown up too many times throughout my life for me to be able to understand a person who says that there is no God. My heart aches and I am burdened when I encounter those who doubt God, who are angry with God or at God, but I understand them based on personal experiences. We cannot comprehend God: It is impossible to wrap our tiny heads around Him. We just overthink. We waste time doubting Him when He is busy designing a blueprint with the most incredible future for us. All we have to do is trust Him and trust the process. It is easier said than done, but that's why it is important to make it a habit. If you are happy, pray. If you are sad, pray. If you are confused, pray. If you are sick, pray. If you are afraid, pray. Believe and pray sincerely. Take time to listen to God. But praying must also be accompanied by action. Sometimes, we have a role to play after praying. God won't appear like Superman and come to the rescue to save you to prove just anything. Still, you will see that when you pray everything shifts and changes. Your life will be restored, the bad will be removed. God works in miraculous ways.

Testimony
Not Green Lentils
By Author

Most children often pray for things they can touch: toys, bicycles, games and shoes. When I was a child, I prayed for food. After my parents separated, my mother was raising my siblings and me on her own, and money was very tight. She had nothing to feed us but green lentils, and that's what we ate every meal. Dad didn't come home for months, mom had nothing left to cook except for a sack of green lentils which was in our pantry. I was famished, but also tired of eating boiled green lentils for breakfast, lunch and dinner. I remember asking God, "Lord, can we have something to eat? Not green lentils, please! I am so hungry but I am tired of eating the same food for every meal."

I remember throwing away the food that mom packed for us for school. I just couldn't keep it down, it was almost a month of eating tasteless food, my tongue would have complained if it had a voice. It was without flavor because there were no other ingredients, just lentils in it. Of course, it was better than nothing, but believe me, it didn't taste good. I would eat it now only because I'm old enough to realize that there are people in the world who eat dirt to fight their hunger pangs. I was too young then, though, to know any better.

My siblings and I attended a Christian Union group meeting in school where Christian kids gathered every Friday in a classroom for praise and worship and fellowship. I so admired the 17-year-old senior students!

I expect I sounded pretty pathetic the day when I quietly told one of the seniors about having no proper meals to eat. I probably said something simple and sad, like, "I am hungry." The next day, this senior student and her dad showed up at my house with fruits and vegetables from their garden. They brought us enough for at least two weeks. I remember the excitement; it felt like Christmas day!

My mom was so thankful, and then the father asked if we had the basic necessities - rice, milk, eggs and so on. She said no. The teenager's dad felt sorry for us, left and came back with lots of provisions. More than just the basics, he even bought us snacks. I remember that day as if it happened yesterday because it was an answered prayer. As a young child, I knew that I could turn to God for anything.

Years passed and we moved away from that town. I lost touch with that senior student. About eight years ago, I found her again through social media. It was such a good feeling to see her profile picture. She didn't look much different. I wrote her a lengthy message explaining how her kind and thoughtful gesture impacted our lives at that time. I thanked her and told her how grateful I was.

She couldn't even remember helping us! Why am I not surprised? Today, this woman is part of a political party that serves women in her community in Malaysia and manages large projects to support single mothers. Her efforts to impact her community are countless. Her late father instilled in her faith and a habit to serve. She is a mother who is a great role model for her children. What an excellent example of a Potter's Child who has been shaped on the wheel of life to benefit people everywhere.

Testimony
See Jane Go, Go Jane Go!
By Jane Rowland

I'm going to share this story because it says in Psalms, I will tell of the wonders of the Lord and I will speak it aloud. It's not because He needs to be reminded. It's because we need to be reminded and somebody here needs to hear this story. So I'm going to tell you this story. But first, to understand it, I need to make sure you know my name. What's my name? It's Jane.

Well, I've been telling this story for thirty years, and I'm 47 years old today.

But back to thirty years ago, it was the spring of 1993, and I was a senior in high school. I was 17 years old and I had grown up in a Christian home. For most of my life I had heard about God speaking, so that was just a normal thing for me. So I can tell you that encouragement, number one, makes it seem possible and normal to your kids that God speaks.

Back to me, I was 17 years old and I knew I had a heart for ministry and a heart for missions. But I just didn't know how I was going to get there. How God was going to lead me in that way. And do you ever have days that you never forget? Yes. This is a day I'll never forget. It was a normal day; I worked at a Bible gift shop in Martinsville, Virginia. I went to Martinsville Christian Fellowship. So it was just a normal day for me at work. And I was closing up shop. And I just remember that whole day, simply feeling this kind of urgency in my spirit, like an anxiousness, less urgency to know what God had for me next. And that day, I just worked like normal, came home from work and it was kind of late. And I looked on my bed, I had a white bedspread. And the only thing sitting on it was a magazine. And I got this magazine several times throughout the year, it was called Campus Life. And it was a Christian magazine for high schoolers and college students. The magazine was sitting on my bed. I remember walking into my room as I said, feeling this urgency to know what God had for me next, and I saw this magazine on my bed. And I said, "God, will you speak to me through this magazine." Just a simple, childlike faith, asking him if he would speak and I went right up to my bed. I closed my eyes, 17-year-old Jane Stettler. I closed my eyes and I opened that magazine. And I didn't fiddle through the pages. I opened my magazine, opened my eyes and a half page ad said, "See Jane go, go Jane, go, you can go to get there with Youth With a Mission in Tyler, Texas. Now, Youth With a Mission was one of the largest Christian missionary organizations in the world. I had barely heard about it. It's short for YWAM, which some of you have heard about. I went running and woke up my parents and said, "I'm going to Texas, and I'm going to live on air."

I was barely 18 years old and my parents sent me off to YWAM. And I got to serve in missions for years. But then, God called us to hear the words my dad said to me before he put me on the plane was you're going to meet your husband.

I was like, "No, I'm gonna be in the jungle translating Bibles." But I did get my husband out of the experience. So it's kind of a jungle at our house or has kind of a jungle vibe. But I just want to encourage you guys that God speaks. I think some of you need to hear today that you do not have a silent father. You might have grown up with one that was silent or maybe didn't show the love or affection or say the words that you needed to hear. But He wants you to know that He is not silent. It says in John (Bible) that my sheep hear my voice. I know them and they follow Me. You are known by the Heavenly Father, by the King of Kings. And he loves you so much. So, I want to encourage you with one more thing that you might make a practice. In the morning, when you wake up, simply say, 'God, I'm listening. Will you speak to me?' And I promise you're going to hear Him speak.

Testimony
A Barren Woman's Prayer
By Author

Have you ever experienced grief where you wished that you could disappear into thin air and be removed from the face of the earth so that you no longer will be consumed by sorrow? Death has a sting many people have experienced, hearing a medical diagnosis for the first time brings intense fear and a mind filled with questions. The word "Cancer" alone causes your entire life to be at a standstill. But what about a barren woman's cry for a child? Can you relate in any way with her? It's not relatable for many; you cannot comprehend her grief. Let me tell you, a woman who longs to be a mother suffers the sting of loss, anguish and a mind flooded with questions; similar to a person diagnosed with a terminal illness. The heartache is unbearable. Infertility snatches away Hope, and without Hope, it's humanly impossible to face another day.

Hope deferred makes the heart sick, but a longing fulfilled is a tree of life. (Proverbs 13:12 NIV)

Throughout life, I have experienced pain and sorrow in many different forms: I would turn to God in prayer, and he would take the pain away; it's almost magical what prayers can do. As a child, when I longed for a dad, he removed the longing, and I no longer needed a father figure. I longed to be loved and respected in a relationship as a woman and prayed to God. He sent me a good husband. Before meeting my husband, my heart was broken when a friend married the boyfriend I'd already introduced to my entire family. I felt betrayed by both my friend and my boyfriend. Two years after they were married, the friend had an affair, and the boyfriend committed suicide. I attended his funeral and closed that chapter behind me with scars and many unanswered questions. Years later, I endured an abusive relationship that left me bruised and broken. Marrying my husband was the best thing that happened to me. He loves me dearly, and I always feel safe and secure with him. Infertility and a failed adoption almost robbed my joy once again. These events brought me to my lowest points in life. It is hard to explain to anyone who has never experienced this pain the grief these episodes can cause, but the power of prayer miraculously healed me.

I prayed for a child, but God didn't do anything about it this time; he seemed quiet as if he had turned his deaf ear to me for a long time. "But why, Lord? Am I going to die?" As silly as that sounds, I asked God such questions because of my past experiences. When my aunt was barren for ten long years, I asked God the same questions, "why aren't you giving her children? She longs to be a mother. She has all the qualities of a mother", I would tell him. "You can make the impossible possible, but why aren't you doing anything? She loves and trusts you, but why are you silent?" I would ask God many questions like a demanding teenager.

I lived with my uncle and aunty for a short period before they passed away. Their prayers for children were never answered. Although I have been to funerals, losing them left a void in my life, and I was shocked. It took me a while to compose myself back, and I almost became numb to pain. My uncle was a heart patient, and my aunty was a cancer patient, he died in January, and my aunty joined him six months later that same year; I had to move out of their house to look for a place to stay. I was in a daze, trying to understand what had happened. But this time, I had answers to all the questions brewing in my head. I remember whispering with a heavy heart, "Lord, I know why you never gave them children; you knew their journey here on earth would be short. They have lived their purpose and taught me life lessons of faith. I will no longer question you, for YOU see the bigger picture." I admired my aunty's faith in God till she breathed her last breath. How can you continue to trust God with a barren womb and as a cancer patient on your deathbed? I witnessed unshaken faith. She wrote, "Life with Christ is an endless hope" in the Bible she presented to me. I mentioned earlier that it's humanly impossible to live without Hope, but she made it clear that with God, we have Hope, and it is possible to live a rich and full life. He would give us joy and peace, the kind only he can give despite our circumstances.

Nobody knew how much I longed for a child because it was not obvious; the desire was almost buried in my heart; it was like a wound that would surface whenever something triggered. I never envied those who had children, but it was heartbreaking to hear remarks that accused me of "trying to replace other moms" or "pretending to like children." I almost stopped being the same person because my intentions were misunderstood. I once prayed to God, asking him to take away my longing for children, and at times, I prayed in agony, like Job did in the Bible. Job was a righteous man who experienced many trials, and at his lowest point in life, he asked if God could take him home. I remember asking God to take me home as I was hurting because I didn't know how to deal with the pain when both my IVF (In vitro fertilization) attempts failed. Somehow, I was able to bounce right back and bury all the desires deep down in the pits of my heart once again. But when my adoption plans fell apart, I was back to where I was; broken beyond repair, so I thought. I decided to leave America, as if that will make the pain go away. One day I woke up to pray, and while reading a devotional, God spoke to me through the message titled "Obedience." The message clearly stated that if I remained in the land God brought me to, he would reveal his "great plans" for me but I will have to trust him through trials and tribulations. He spoke through that message when I was almost close to purchasing a ticket to go back to Malaysia for a long break. I immediately had peace in my heart. My feet were in a hurry to skip and hop again, so I dressed up to go out to Hobby Lobby with a purpose. I purchased a sign for my closet, "It Is Well With My Soul."

Inspirational words, quotes and books always lifted my spirits up, I took a glimpse of that sign every morning, assuring myself that it is well. The following day my friend invited me to the Propel Women's Conference; I gladly attended it that weekend. I cannot begin to describe how God showed up on that day to talk to me, and it was as if he orchestrated that entire conference for me alone. The first song was "It Is Well With My Soul." For the first time, I heard the story of the song's writer and the deep meaning of those words. I sat in my car after the conference and cried like a baby for almost two hours. I realized that the packed parking lot was empty when I gained consciousness. I was afraid that the security officer would approach me with a suspicious look, so I drove home quickly. When I reached home, there was a large package on the couch. "What is this?" I asked my husband. "Oh, it's a housewarming gift from Pastor Biju," he said. When I opened it, I almost fell on my face in disbelief. You wouldn't believe this; it was a beautiful square black wooden decorative piece with white words written, "When peace like a river attendeth my way, when sorrows like sea billows roll, whatever my lot, thou hast taught me to say, it is well, it is well with my soul." I sobbed, ran to my closet, held my sign in one hand, and started speed talking like a bullet train to my husband about the message, the signage, the conference, the first song, and God showing up. My husband just looked at me; I probably looked like a crazy woman rambling or behaving like Hannah in the Bible where people thought she was drunk although she was simply praying.

How do I explain to you how God showed up and blessed me with twins years later after I told him it was well with my soul? Where do I begin? I prayed, "Lord, let your will be done, your desires for me, not mine. You alone are enough; I will settle for two puppies, but can you please help me by removing the desire for children in my heart? My heart hurts, it will make it easier to heal", I told him. He never removed the desire from my heart because he knew I wanted to be a mother more than anything. I loved children. God alone knew my real heart; he made me that way and gave me the desires; he had plans to fulfill them in his time. When I first found out that I was pregnant, it was almost surreal, two? God gave me two precious babies, a boy, and a girl. Only he can! His ways are not ours; his answers may not come when we expect them, but he comes through somehow, in his time. He sees the bigger picture, and you have to trust him with your life.

As I raise my twins, I can attest to the power of prayer and the joy it restores. In life, we will have tribulations, but we can only bounce back and face life stronger by looking up to God each time we fall. I can never face a day without God; you don't have to if you pick up the prayer habit. But, friend, there is a difference, as the famous poem reminds us.

The Difference

I got up early one morning and rushed right into the day.

I had so much to accomplish that I didn't have time to pray.

Problems just tumbled about me, and heavier came each task.

"Why doesn't God help me?" I wondered.

He answered, "You didn't ask,"

I wanted to see joy and beauty, but the day toiled on, gray and bleak.

I wondered why God didn't show me. He said, "But you

didn't seek."

I tried to come into God's presence. I used all my keys at the lock.

God gently and lovingly chided, "My child, you didn't knock."

I woke up early this morning and paused before entering the day.

I had so much to accomplish that I had to take time to pray.

Alan Grant

Testimony
A Single Mom's Cry
By Sharon Patricia D'cruz

Sharon Patricia grew up in a single-parent home, then fled her own abusive marriage to protect her children. She says that she was able to rely on God through her difficult years:

Growing up without the presence of a father, I yearned to be loved just like any young adult. My journey of rocky roads continued after a rough childhood and episodes of traumatic teenage years.

In younger years, I was rejected romantically by one because I lacked a college degree. By another because I had a "dirty" skin tone. Yet again, because I came from a "broken family" with no idea where my father had gone 29 years earlier.

To be marriage-worthy requires meeting so many demands! I thought. I was sticking by all the right rules but nothing was still good enough to be accepted, to be included, or to be loved.

I fell in love naively. I trusted everybody at face value and was hopelessly gullible, only to be taken advantage of. I took the wrong road and got mangled in an abusive relationship. We had two kids, but the abuse continued ten times worse - abuse in every aspect, you can imagine!

So I fled and hid away with my children for ten years from that volatile relationship.

One thing remained firm throughout those moments of rejection, confusion, fear, despair, loneliness, torture and trauma -- my firm faith in Christ Jesus my Savior. My only source of strength was drawn from reading the Psalms out loud in the confines of my apartment in the wee hours of the morning. Tears were my morning offerings and my broken life was all I had to offer God.

Neither isolation nor financial barriers could keep me from attending church or purchasing praise and worship CDs and DVDs. I sang crying and laughing at the same time. I sang praises through all my challenging times, believing and trusting that God would turn all my mourning into dancing, as the Bible says (Psalms 30:11). I did what I could to be the best mother and father to both my children.

I told God that He was my first love and He will always be. At the same time, I reasoned with God that I'm still human. I kept praying for a human life partner who would keep my children and me safe and loved. I wanted a complete family with a father for my children, a husband-best friend for me.

I was a single mother with children for ten years with barely enough to live comfortably, hiding from my ex who was constantly stalking and threatening. I kept to my faith and that kept me going forward. God reminded me of His favor and His faithfulness towards single women in the Bible: Hagar, Leah, and Ruth[1]. He gave me promises, and made a way. In 2017, God changed my circumstances and brought an understanding partner and a loving father for my children.

God saw, heard, and knew my situation. He had spoken to me through the biblical story of Joshua in 2006[2] and He is still walking with me and my family till this very second. No words are enough to describe God's love, peace and faithfulness in my family life.

We are now serving in two ministries as a family in Australia and evangelizing to those who don't know Jesus Christ.

Look around you. Do you see an answered prayer? If you believe in the power of prayer, you will be able to start listing your answered prayers.

Testimony
A Pair of Shoes
By Binu Samuel

Devotional author Binu Samuel tells this story about the time a man's prayer caught her husband's attention in a crowd.

We walked out of the sanctuary and into our church's main lobby. I thought my husband was headed toward our usual corner where we typically chat with a few friends after service. But my husband veered off to a different side of the lobby. When I spotted him, I noticed his arm was around the shoulder of a fellow church attendee. The two appeared engrossed in a deep conversation.

As we drove home, I couldn't help but ask what that conversation was all about.

My husband filled me in: "During the service, I noticed that man's socks. I noticed his socks because of the holes he had in his shoes. I felt a strong nudge in my heart to buy the man a pair of shoes... - so I was asking the man his shoe size."

We've attended this church for over twenty years. It's a fairly large congregation with multiple service times, so meeting new people was nothing new for my husband. But walking up to someone he has never spoken to before and asking him his shoe size? Now that was a first.

I continued my questioning: "Oh, wow... - was he surprised? Was he insulted? Does he simply like his old shoes?"

My husband replied, "No, he wasn't insulted at all. His eyes filled up, and his chin quivered. He was actually moved. I gave him my number and asked him to call me. I told him I'd like to meet up with him at the mall."

Two days later, my husband and the man met. There, in the food court, this man shared his story. A few poor choices had led him to where he was. He was thankful for a stable job, but he still had a long way to go.

He told my husband, "I don't do well with handouts. I accepted your offer because I knew it was God. I have a funeral to attend later this week. This past Sunday morning when you approached me, I had just looked through my closet to see if I had a pair of shoes decent enough to wear to the funeral. I didn't. So I asked God that morning if He could somehow provide a pair of shoes. When you asked my shoe size, I knew God had heard my prayer. I was overwhelmed by God."

After purchasing the shoes, my husband asked his new friend if there was anything else he needed.

"No, thank you," his friend replied. "I'm good. I just asked God for shoes."

Perhaps you find yourself alone and in need. Maybe your choices or the choices of others have led you to this place. It doesn't matter. God still hears you. Even those quiet, desperate prayers you pray alone in your closet, God hears.

Our God will drop everything. He will leave the ninety-nine. He will even tug at the hearts of His children to care for the needs of the one.

Testimony
Lost Documents
By Author

Weekends are usually "laundry and tidy up" days in our house. As I was rushing to get chores done before heading out to my job, my husband frantically told me that he had misplaced some crucial documents. These documents held our future. The envelope he'd lost contained a stack of copies he'd compiled as part of his package to accept a job. He had to send them immediately to meet the deadline. He was about to head out to the UPS store with the envelope, but he couldn't find it anywhere in the house. His job and our future were at stake.

I told him that I was getting ready to go to my own job, but would be back later to help him look for it. He said, "No, you have to help me find it, or I won't have a job, please don't go to work." I told him that it was too late to call in since it wouldn't be possible to get someone to fill in on such short notice. He kept saying in a panicky voice that we had to look for his documents. I then said, "Sweetheart, let's pray."

"Pray!??" he said. "I have been looking for these documents since morning." I can't remember if he rolled his eyes, but I know he thought I was crazy to turn to prayer at that point.

As crazy as it sounds, miracles do happen! I held his hands, bowed my head and started praying. I asked God to help us find the documents. I asked Him to give us the peace we needed, I thanked God for the future he was planning for us. I expressed my belief that the job my husband had applied for was the plan God had in His blueprint of our lives. When I ended the prayer, I shook my husband's arms and said, " I am going to work, but I promise you that I won't go to bed until we find the documents today." I remember the blank stare he gave me. That look which said, "You seriously think this is going to make a difference?"

Hardly two minutes later, I heard my husband run up the stairs calling for me.

"I... - I found it!" he panted. "I found it!" The envelope had lodged under the sliding table where the computer keyboard sat.

I started sobbing profusely. These were not happy tears, nor sad tears, but I was sobbing because he had doubted the power of prayer. I held his hands and said while crying: "Sweetheart, you have to believe! You have to believe that we have a miracle working God. It hurts me that you doubted - it hurts me that you don't believe. He can make the impossible possible, but you have to believe."

I remember how my husband stood still and just looked at me. I don't know what he was thinking, I just hoped that he realized we have a miracle working God. My husband loves Jesus just as much as I do and he trusts Him, even though this was just a "doubting Thomas" moment.

I have questioned God many times myself, especially when my IVF (In vitro fertilization) attempts failed twice. So, even if you're in uncertain circumstances, "say a prayer and go to bed." God doesn't sleep or slumber. He is constantly working on shaping your life like a potter who shapes the clay on the wheel.

Testimony
Struggling with Suicide
By Me Ra Koh

Even when living with the worst possible suffering, it's possible to take steps forward. Me Ra Koh tells her story of beating back the emotional trauma and lying voices that nearly led her to suicide after she was raped, stalked, ridiculed in court, and lived terrified for months in her car.

For those Struggling with Suicide.
This is My Story.

One of my greatest medals in life may seem shameful to others, but I wear it with pride. I earned it from the season I was struggling with suicide, tormented by all its lies, and didn't give in. I know joy. But I know even more what it means to be desperate. I know what it's like to scream with all your might and yet not a sound comes out. No one can hear you. If you have never heard me speak or visited my About Me page on my website, you may not know there was a time in my life when I wanted to end it all. A victim of date rape. Ridiculed by the courts. Unable to go home. Stalked. Terrified. I lived out of my car for months and heard the invitation of suicide every day.

The Lies Said ...

"You'd make everyone's life easier if you weren't here." "You have nothing to live for." "No one will really understand how much you're hurting unless you end it all. Then they will know. And then they will regret not doing more." Along with, "You're damaged goods." "Pain is your past, pain is your present, and pain is your future." "Why fight so hard?" "You've been through so much. You've done enough. You deserve the break." "You can only take so much pain. Why not end it all?" These were only some of the lies that shadowed me every day and every long sleepless night.

The Biggest Hurdle with Emotional Trauma

The biggest hurdle with emotional trauma and pain is that no one can see it. It's like we've been in a life-threatening car accident on an emotional level. We are in the middle of the street bleeding on the inside. But no one comes running. No one calls the ambulance. Since no one can see it or validate the pain, we choose to ignore it, too. But unacknowledged pain isolates us.

Shame Taunts Us with Feelings of Failure

Within this isolation, I almost lost the battle to suicide thirty years ago. I almost believed my life was worthless. And in one last, desperate act to survive, to scream and be heard, I checked myself into a locked psychiatric ward. You see, suicide had become such a fierce, mental bully, I didn't believe I could be trusted to be alone anymore. I have never felt so utterly shattered in my life. But the moment we acknowledge we can't do this life on our own is the moment we step toward healing.

That Is When Life Begins

One of the hardest parts of our healing process is that we are the only ones who can ask for help. We're the only ones who know how much we're silently hurting, struggling with suicide. We're the only ones that can call the suicide hotline, reach out to a friend, pastor, or counselor, or even willingly admit ourselves into a psych ward. And we know, as shameful as struggling with suicide feels, we cannot be trusted to be alone because the option of suicide is too real.

Struggling with suicide became even more fierce once my friend killed himself.

I had been a patient in the psychiatric ward for a month. Each day, though, had brought deeper healing. My release papers were being drawn up. And then my counselor asked to speak with me. There had been so much trauma and pain to work through in that psych ward. But when my counselor told me my closest friend had committed suicide, I literally thought I was having a heart attack. My heart physically hurt. With hands pressed to my chest, I crumbled to the floor and began wailing. The fight to go on had just become a thousand times more difficult.

Suddenly, the voices of suicide had shifted. "If he didn't hang in there, why do you have to?" "See, it's not that big of a deal." "He's not hurting anymore." "You can be free of all this pain, too."

But there was another side.

I had now experienced the trauma of losing someone to suicide. I knew firsthand how it turns your life and heart upside down. The first few months are like a blur. Everything in you feels numb. You think you see the person in a crowd. You follow a stranger into a mall. You're sure that it must be them because you still can't believe they're gone.

Throughout all of this, can I tell you one of the most powerful truths I've learned?

My friend's suicide showed me how his tragic decision didn't fix anything. Instead, he left his friends and family in a wake of unbelievable pain. He believed a lie that everything would be better if he was gone. The exact opposite was true. It took years for his family and friends to recover.

The most courageous and difficult thing you'll ever do is face your pain, embrace it, and lead it to healing. But it always, always starts with us. It is the single step only we can take. If you're hurting, be the one that tells someone how much you're hurting. Be the first one to validate your pain by asking for help. You deserve a champion in your life. Be the champion for yourself, your heart, on this real battlefield of life and death.

You are not alone.

No matter what the voices are telling you, you are not alone. God will meet you. He is for you, not against you. Myself and other warriors are fighting for you in prayer and choosing to never accept shame again. Through my own healing journey, I have discovered the truth about those lies. And now I cheer you on. I wear my battle scars with pride, sharing my story, inviting you to do the same. My heart is turned upward in thanks for the Medal of Life because I know how hard I fought to overcome the lies. There were countless times when the battle seemed impossible, the pain too much to bear. But we must still risk believing that all the lies aren't real. Shame is never the truth. And hope was, and is, still alive.

The Kind of Awards Dinner I Want to Host Someday . . .

Every year I see awards dinners and events on television. One day I'd like to host an awards dinner for all of us who have faced our demons and lived to tell of life on the other side. What a powerful gathering it would be. What stories we will share. If you're in a desperate place, I want you to be at that awards dinner someday. There is a seat at the table with your name on it. Will you choose to fight today, to ask for help, so you can join me and so many others at that dinner someday?

To read more of Me Ra Koh's story, see her books *Beauty Restored: Finding Life and Hope After Date Rape and 4 Minutes to Hear God's Voice* at https://fioria.us/ books or on Amazon.

Excerpt reprinted with permission from Me Ra Koh's blog; https://fioria.us/blog/

If you are struggling with suicidal feelings, you

may want to seek support from one of the 24/7 resources available, in addition to resources offered at your church and among Christian friends.

Telephone hotlines are staffed by volunteers and paid professionals around the world. This list references only the numbers in countries named in this text. Others may be located online at https://blog.opencounseling.com/suicide-hotlines/.

US	988
India	8888817666
Malaysia	06-2842500
UK	0800 689 5652
Ireland	+4408457909090

A crisis text line provides confidential chats in four countries:

US/Canada	741741
UK	85258
Ireland	50808

How to Pray The Lord's Prayer
By Dr. Paul Dhinakaran

I am grateful to Dr. Paul Dhinakaran of Jesus Calls
Ministry, based in Chennai, Tamil Nadu, India, for
permission to share with you this guidance he provides
for effective prayer.

The Lord says that we should all pray the prayer which He taught the disciples, which is found in Matthew 6:9-13 (ESV), "Pray then like this: 'Our Father in heaven, hallowed be your name. Your kingdom come, your will be done, on earth as it is in heaven. Give us this day our daily bread, and forgive us our debts, as we also have forgiven our debtors, And lead us not into temptation, but deliver us from evil."

The Lord says we should begin the prayer with "Our Father in heaven." Every time Jesus prayed, He said "Father." Even today, that is what the Lord wants us to do—we need to call on our Father. Although there are different ways in which we address God when we pray, like: "O Lord, our Rock," etc., the fact remains that He is our Father. We address God as "our Father" because when we address God as our Father, it immediately connects the ones for whom we are praying to God, making God their Father, too. Further, He is going to be Father to each one of us and to everyone for whom we pray. God is our Abba, appa, papa, or daddy! We are grateful to the Holy Spirit for revealing this truth to us.

As a Father, He is moved with compassion towards everyone. So let us cry out to Him and say, "Father, heal me, Father, save me, Father, deliver me," and He will!

In 2 Corinthians 6:18, God says, "I will be a Father to you, and you will be my sons and daughters, says the Lord Almighty." In a worldly sense, we are happy, sometimes even thrilled, to introduce our sons and daughters, saying, "This is my son/daughter . . ." The Lord says that He is going to rejoice over you, saying, "This is My daughter, this is My son!" He is going to prove to the world that you are His daughter/son, so let us pray, "Our Father in heaven."

In Psalm 86:11 the Psalmist says, "Teach me Your way, Lord; that I may rely on Your faithfulness..." He is going to teach us His ways this year because He is our Father. The Bible says in Isaiah 54:13, "all your children will be taught by the Lord, and great will be their peace." I believe this is what God said about Israel, that the children in Israel shall be taught by the Lord. All of us are the children of the Almighty God, whether we are in our 80's or 90's; God doesn't have grandchildren.

Once you start addressing Him as "Father,'" He will begin to teach you and your children. And the result? All will experience great peace. What a blessing it is to experience great peace in these days of turmoil! Gear up to experience such peace this year.

Moreover, the Lord's watchful eyes will be on us, according to His promise in Psalm 32:8 – I will guide you with My eye. This promise is interwoven with the promise in Isaiah 58:11, "The Lord will guide you always; he will satisfy your needs in a sun-scorched land and will strengthen your frame. You will be like a well-watered garden, like a spring whose waters never fail."

Always Pray and Never Give Up

With such great promises to fall back on, we are called to "pray without ceasing" as recorded in 1 Thessalonians. 5:17. In Luke chapter 18, Jesus encourages His disciples to pray without giving up and quotes the example of the persistent appeal of a widow to her judge, and how that unjust judge granted her request.

My father, D.G.S. Dhinakaran, taught us this: "Pray always, pray continuously, and pray for everything." I urge you to pray when you sit down and when you stand up; when you enter an auditorium and when you leave, pray; when the phone rings let your prayer be, "Lord, this caller should be blessed with miracles; give me the revelation to pray for the caller.' Likewise, when you hear a prayer request, immediately pray. And God will teach you and guide you with the right answer, and you shall have that great peace. This peace will be passed on to the person requesting prayers.

Pray when you send your children to school. Pray when your spouse goes to his/her office. When you start to pray before, pray during and pray after whatever you are asking for. Then you will see the Father giving you "great peace" in everything. Jesus is our "Everlasting Father," as revealed in Isaiah 9. All of us are the children of the Everlasting Father; so we cry to him, "Teach me your way Father, that I may rely on your faithfulness, I am unfaithful but you are faithful,'" as stated in 2 Timothy 2:13, "If we are faithless, he remains faithful, for he cannot disown himself."

The Undivided Heart

Our prayer, as we progress should be along the lines of Psalm 86, "give me an undivided heart, O Lord, that I may fear your name; I want to know your ways, so that I will not have double standards, but that I will be able to fear your name and revere your name, O Lord.' He is our Father and so we need to revere and fear Him. There should be no such thing as my Father's ways and my ways; it is only the Father's ways. Our prayer should be, "Not my way, nor my will, but let Thy will be done, dear Father," exactly as Jesus prayed. Then God will open His ways to us and fulfill His will, and we will have the fear of God. Look how Jacob addressed God in Genesis 31:42, "If the God of my father, the God of Abraham and the Fear of Isaac had not been . . ." That is how your children should call God, keeping you as a model. Yes they should be able to say, "My father's God is the fear of my father (and/or mother, as the case may be)." God says He will teach us His ways, and will give us the grace to walk with an undivided heart to fear His name.

". . . for you who revere my name, the sun of righteousness will rise with healing in its rays. And you will go out and frolic like well-fed calves. Then you will trample on the wicked; they will be ashes under the soles of your feet on the day when I act," says the Lord Almighty." – Malachi 4:2-3

"Teach me your way, Lord, that I may rely on your faithfulness; give me an undivided heart, that I may fear your name," (Psalm 86:11b).

When you give to the Lord your undivided heart, it results in your ability to "trample on the wicked" and you develop a reverential way of "fearing the Name of the Lord." Therefore, there is no need to fear the evil one but to increase in the fear of the Lord. Remember, the fear of the Lord is the beginning of wisdom. Be honest in paying your taxes; be accountable in handling your finances, prompt in paying your bills. Set your household in order, be faithful in supporting one another and walk humbly before God. Be careful with your words. Do not spread/forward scandals and rumors. Along the lines of 1 Thessalonians 4:11, "Mind your own business, lead a quiet life, and work with your hands." You will then frolic like well-fed calves.

The Fire of God

In 1 Kings 18:21, before Elijah brought fire down from heaven, he addressed all the people of Israel, the prophets of Baal and the king of Israel, crying out to them, "How long will you waver between two opinions? If the Lord is God, follow Him; but if Baal is God, follow him." You cannot linger between two opinions. We need to make an intentional choice to follow the God who answers by fire.

In Luke 12:49, when Jesus came into the world, He says, "I have come to bring fire upon the earth . . ." Another translation (NLT) says, "I have come so that I can set the world on fire," because fire is the nature of God. In the Old Testament days, God Almighty was a consuming fire. Ezekiel 8:2 says that God had fire burning below his waist, and above the waist it was molten metal; yes, that is God.

For us to bring fire down from heaven to consume the works of the evil one, we need to go through the baptism of fire, as recorded in Acts 2:4. John Wesley said, "When you set yourself on Fire, people love to come and see you burn!"

When you follow the Lord your Father with all your heart, the fire of God will be on you, making the image of God visible in you. This, in turn, will draw people to God. Let us cry out to the Lord for this grace—grace to love the Lord your God with all you heart, no double standards—it is not "world and Jesus"; it's just Jesus and Jesus alone. He is our Father. Just close your eyes and visualize the image of the Father—fire; and you are to reflect this image in your life. Can you now see in your mind's eye that you are on fire? Can you see how this connects with John Wesley's words, "People will love to come and see you burn"?

Shall we cry out for this fire right now? Let's put our hands on our chest, and say, "Lord, I open my heart totally to you, Lord, one hundred percent for Jesus; my heart should not be a divided heart this year, Lord, no double standards, Lord, only Jesus and Jesus alone. As He is in heaven so shall I be on earth. Amen." Be assured, His grace is descending on you right now.

Hallowed Be Thy Name

Hallowed means sacred and holy, therefore, we are called to revere and respect the One to whom this prayer is addressed. Proverbs 30:9 says, "Otherwise, I may have too much and disown you and say, 'Who is the Lord?' Or I may become poor and steal, and so dishonor the name of my

God." This verse depicts two extremes—the wealthy and the poverty stricken; the ones who say, "Why do I need God?" and the other group that says, "Let us steal, this is the only way to survive." The reason behind both reactions is lack of trust in God's providence, and both groups are dishonoring God.

A story is told about an old woman who thanked God every day for her food. One day two mischievous boys dropped a loaf of bread down the chimney and ran around and knocked on the door. Meanwhile, the woman took the loaf and said, "Thank you, Jesus." When she opened the door the boys asked her, "Do you know who gave you that bread?" and she replied cheerfully, "Jesus!"

No matter through what channel your needs are met, be sure to give thanks to God, for He can use any channel to provide for you. Remember Elijah and the ravens! Our duty is to hallow the name of Jesus.

Thy Kingdom Come, Thy Will Be Done

"For the kingdom of God is not eating and drinking, but righteousness and peace and joy in the Holy Spirit," Romans 14:17.

God has already made plans for us, as per Jeremiah 29:11, and Romans 8:26-27 assures us that the Holy Spirit

". . . helps in our weaknesses. For we do not know what we should pray for as we ought, but the Spirit Himself intercedes for us with groanings which cannot be uttered . . "

When we are praying in the Spirit, God makes us prophesy those plans of God again. We find this in Revelation 10:7 and 11: ". . . but in the days of the sounding of the seventh angel, when he is about to sound, the mystery of God would be finished, as He declared to His servants the prophets." And verse 11, ". . . he said to me, 'You must prophesy again about many peoples, nations, tongues, and kings.'" Yes, this is the prayer that God wants us to pray, "let your will be downloaded into me, Lord, that I may prophesy and fulfill your will on earth." When we prophesy, our prayer goes up as incense to God, and it mixes with the blood of Jesus Christ in heaven, which is also interceding, and when the incense and the blood mixes together it becomes fire, and the answer comes like fire from heaven, which is explained in Revelation 8:3-5. We are going to get answers as fire from heaven. Amen!

Give Us Today Our Daily Bread

God provided manna in the wilderness to sustain His children. If food is important for the body, how much more is spiritual food for the soul? Yes, man shall not live by bread alone, but by every word that comes from the mouth of God, explains Deuteronomy 8:3 and Matthew 4:4.

Let us pray and ask the Lord to help us not miss Bible reading even for a single day this year. When you read the Bible, hear the voice of the Lord speaking to you. Because only what God reveals to you in the morning will be the power of God for your family, and the thousands who would come to you for prayer. So we pray, "Lord, give us this day our daily bread."

Forgive Us Our Sins as We Forgive Those Who Sin Against Us

In the words of Jesus we have a clear definition of what this part of the Lord's Prayer means: "For if you forgive men their trespasses, your Heavenly Father will also forgive you. But if ye do not forgive, neither will your Father which is in heaven forgive your trespasses," (Matthew 6:14-15). There is a link between forgiveness and healing; when you forgive from the depths of your heart, you will overcome the bitterness on the one who wronged you. Therefore, the stress is released. Stress, you know, is the cause for most physical and psychological ailments. Apostle James affirms this, "Therefore confess your sins to each other and pray for each other so that you may be healed," (James 5:16a).

When our relationship with God and people (vertical and horizontal) is on the right track, its result makes our ministry more meaningful. We begin to think of the needs of others in different spheres. We move on from spiritual help to meeting the physical, intellectual, and social needs of people around us.

Lead Us Not Into Temptation, But Deliver Us from Evil

Yes, we are giving and forgiving and thus, pleasing God. When all is going well, that's when Satan entices us with evil desires. James 1: 14 explains, ". . . but each person is tempted when they are dragged away by their own evil desire and enticed." But thanks be to God for the promise in 1 Corinthians 10:13, "No temptation has overtaken you except such as is common to man; but God is faithful, who will not allow you to be tempted beyond what you are able, but with the temptation will also make the way of escape, that you may be able to bear it."

The prayer, "deliver us from evil," is answered when God turns temptations into testing, so that like Job "we shall come forth as gold," (Job 23:10). This is the way of escape that He shows us. And the outcome is gold! This gold is not the material gold; it is the presence of the living God in us and working through us. As each of you are engaged in carrying others in prayer, this gold—the presence of God—will flow through you to them. Jesus is revealed to others through us. Can anything be more precious than this?

For Thine Is the Kingdom and the Power and the Glory, Forever and Ever, Amen

My dear people of God, Jesus explains in Luke 17:10 that we are unprofitable servants and we have done our duty, and the glory goes to God. Let us all turn to our Father right now and pray the Lord's Prayer meaningfully.

Our Father in heaven, Hallowed be Your name. Your kingdom come. Your will be done on earth as it is in heaven. Give us this day our daily bread. And forgive us our debts, as we forgive our debtors. And do not lead us into temptation, but deliver us from the evil one. For Yours is the kingdom and the power and the glory forever. Amen.

Habits to Practice

When you keep track of what you ask God, you can see what happens. It doesn't need to be complicated, and you certainly don't need to be careful how you write. This habit is simply about keeping notes that you can look back at later to remind yourself that God is present to help you in need and to encourage you when you're sad or afraid.

Different people keep track of their prayers and the answers in different ways. I keep a prayer list with names, dates and requests on sticky notes. I write about goals that I want to accomplish, a friend who is sick, someone who is going through a divorce, infertility struggles, exams, etc. At times my list is short, but most of the time my list takes up an entire large sticky note, even in tiny writing. I always have more than twenty prayer items. So if you ask me to pray for you, be well assured that you are on my list.

When I write a new list, I fold the earlier list up as if I was getting ready to pick a lucky draw, and tuck it into the pockets of my Bible cover. Every now and then I open one to read and discover answered prayers after months or even years. In March 2018, I wrote "#18 - Twins - A boy and a girl" under "my heart's desires." I rediscovered the note when I was pregnant with my twins and had just completed a pregnancy photo shoot. I was in awe, shocked, and I remember shedding tears of joy. It was almost surreal because I couldn't even remember writing it. I had been so ready to settle for puppies during my third IVF (In vitro fertilization) attempt, and I'd even told my husband that he would come home to two puppies if my blood test came back negative. Instead, I purchased two life-size baby balloons with a welcome sign which said, "We can't wait to see you daddy." I even shared pictures of the sticky note prayer with the couple who took my portraits.

So write down your list today, and start praying about it. God's answers are not always "yes" to all your requests, but

His answers are designed beautifully just for you. He knows you best; you have to trust His plans for you and your life.

Habits to Teach Children

Make a prayer list together with your children. Be transparent with them in some areas of your life, so you will allow your children to see how prayer can work. If my mom had never shared her faith about the financial burden she had with me and my siblings, we would have never seen the miracles that took place in our lives. Children learn faith through your experiences when they are young. There will be other instances where your child's answered prayer strengthens your faith and beliefs. Faith is a gift, and studies have proven that those who have faith in God are happier, more successful and stronger mentally and emotionally.

Your family prayer list with your children could be as simple as this:

Date	Asked	Answered	Date of answer
9/26/20	Help Mom finish this big work project on time!	Wow! It's done	9/28/20
9/26/20	Help daughter study well for social studies test	Good work! A B+, which is better than last test	10/1/20

Date	Asked	Answered	Date of answer
9/26/20	Help son find friends who will encourage him, not bullies	He's been invited to go to a Rotary event by someone he knows at school	10/18/20
9/27/20	Encourage daughter about not having made the team	She's getting interested in trying the math team (!!) instead	11/2/20
9/27/20	Son wants new sneakers more like friends have		

Talking with children about how God nudges you in the right direction when you ask for help will help them to recognize not just the answered prayer, but how God leads us when we ask for God's help.

Busy pediatrician Dr. Elizabeth R. Thomas and her husband have found prayer as a family is an important part of their daily household routine. The co-author of *Quest for More* says:

These days, when we come home exhausted after a full day of work, tackling sports schedules and showers for the kids, my husband and I have a major decision to make before we both hit the pillow: How are we going to end our evening?

No matter how much we want to crawl into bed, we choose family prayer. Yes, there are days we do short ones, but most days, we make an effort to sit in the family room with our Bibles, discuss a passage, and have each person pray.

The other night while we were sitting for family prayer, we came across this verse: "But if serving the Lord seems undesirable to you, then choose for yourselves this day whom you will serve, whether the gods your ancestors served beyond the Euphrates, or the gods of the Amorites, in whose land you are living. But as for me and my household, we will serve the Lord." Joshua 24:15

It hit me right there.

Since my husband and I have made a conscious decision to make prayer a priority, I know for a fact that it will not only bless my children, but also their children and grandchildren. I want my great great great grandchildren to love Jesus.

But much of that responsibility lies on the choices I make today. Family prayer may seem like a mundane task. It isn't.

It's challenging to teach young children how to respect time in God's presence. Sometimes giggles ensue and become contagious. Other times, they get easily distracted and lose focus.

Despite the obstacles, I know that they will learn to respect and enjoy their time with Jesus as they mature. Prioritizing family prayer now will have an incredible impact on their future . . . not only for my children but also for the generations that follow.

Chapter 2

Make Your Bed
(Get the Job Done!)

So when you fold the sheets and make your bed,

You unfold the day, you step ahead,

With your head held high, a sparkle in your eye,

You learn afresh something you never can deny.

For what you do is what makes the most of you,

And what you think is what sparks the passion in you,

So start your day right, like the sun that shines bright always,

These little habits that you embrace will embrace you back with more grace!

Susan Ann Samuel

What is the first task you do when you wake up? What is the last thing you do before you go to sleep?

For a minute, imagine walking into your bedroom after a long, exhausting day. You see your comfortable bed, its neatly tucked sheets and fluffed pillows inviting you to rest. You lay down, and it smells of the lavender fragrance you bought while shopping for groceries, the fragrance that comes with a softener that turns ordinary linens to soft feather-like comfort. It feels like heaven, and you sleep in the clouds.

Will it matter to you that you made your bed this morning? Maybe not. Perhaps you were never bothered if you had to jump into a rumpled bed with dirty sheets and flat pillows. Even with cookie crumbs all over your sleeping space, you sleep as soundly as a baby, you say.

Habit No. 2: Make Your Bed is not about the comfort of the bed or whether it's immaculate. This habit is rather about making the bed; the task itself. Something about making the bed in the morning sets the tone that begins the day in order. You wake up and complete the first task even though you had a choice to skip the job. By doing it, you prepare yourself mentally to get things done. It is a habit, so you don't sweat doing it; your subconscious mind knows your pattern and your hands begin to get the job done right away.

If you prefer coming home to a made bed then it's a big win. If it doesn't matter to you, you have still taken the day's first important step toward achieving higher skills. If you have served in the military or worked in the hospitality industry, you have learned that making the bed is of great importance. The reason may be different, yet the lesson is almost the same: it creates order and tidiness. Author Charles Duhigg, in his book The Power of Habit, stated "making your bed every morning is correlated with better productivity, a greater sense of well-being, and stronger skills at sticking with a budget." Admiral William H. McRaven emphasizes the importance of simple habits when he says, "If you want to change the world, start off by making your bed."

If you want to change the world,

Start Off By Making Your Bed.

"If you make your bed every morning,

you will have accomplished the first task of the day.

It will give you a small sense of pride and

it will encourage you to do another task and another and another.

By the end of the day, that one task completed

will have turned into many tasks completed.

Making your bed will also reinforce the fact that

little things in life matter.

If you can't do the little things right,
you will never do the big things right."

Admiral William McRaven

2014 Commencement Address
University of Texas, Austin [3]

Set Yourself Up for Success, One Task at a Time

It's not all about making a bed, of course. The bed that's made is just the first thing that you've finished. It sets your mind up to finish something else. When you always finish the first task of the day, it's easier to go forward completing others.

Physician-Scientist Dr. Sanya Thomas says that accomplishing this task as soon as you're up and about immediately brings clarity and focus. Beyond that, she urges that people develop a daily morning ritual. The sequence of actions could include praying, making your bed, making yourself a cup of hot drink, meditating, or engaging in a physical activity. This could be followed by reviewing your to-do list for the day and triaging its various tasks, based on priority. Keeping the day's task list short will prove highly valuable in adult life when most agenda items are complicated enough to take several hours, or even days, to finish. Once you've prioritized your tasks, you can plan the rest of your day to accommodate them into your schedule. Complicated tasks would often need to be broken down into smaller chunks, and blocking time throughout the day to overcome your hardest challenges ensures progress in the right direction. Early risers make the most of this kind of ritual, and you'll be full of positive energy for the rest of your day once you've mastered disciplining your morning routine.

Some people say discipline is key to success. How do you define discipline? The disciplinary process is a necessity in achieving goals and success. Forget about big things, even if you want to achieve a small project you still need discipline to complete it. You either have it or you don't, and it's a struggle to face life without the habit of discipline.

Although challenging, discipline can be mastered when you make it a habit. Once mastered, this habit will serve you well in everything you do. You will be able to endure the challenges and hurdles that come on your way when you are trying to get a task done. It's will power — a must-have habit.

In my experience, discipline is not a natural phenomenon. It's a learned process, it has to be a verb first before it is a noun. A verb represents an action. A noun represents an object - person, place, or thing. Discipline begins with an action before it becomes a habit or character.

One of my brothers-in-law shared a meaningful sermon in his church about discipline, including a poem which is fit for a potter's child. He said, "The more God wants to use you, the more he will discipline you first." It's the same with our children. When we correct them or reprimand them to do what is right, it's only because we want to mold and shape them to be good and do good. We have to endure tantrums and cries, unfortunately that's part of the disciplinary process. Often, it hurts us more to see them hurt. My uncle, who was the disciplinarian in my family when I was growing up, shared on my 40th birthday that his heart ached whenever he had to discipline me. I only remember that he taught me many valuable habits that mattered more than moments when he reprimanded me for my wrong actions.

When we disobey our parents, teachers, or authorities, we have to be prepared to face the consequences for our actions. The consequences can be time outs, suspension, termination, fines, tickets, or other serious consequences like imprisonment. In our day-to-day life, consequences of bad habits will show up as friction with family members, friends, and peers. We can also suffer bad grades, serious medical conditions, separation and divorce, and other forms of struggles if we don't change our ways. We are not in control of certain aspects of our lives, but for the most part our choices good and bad determine the quality of our lives.

When God Wants To Drill A Man

When God wants to drill a man,

And thrill a man,

And skill a man

When God wants to mold a man

To play the noblest part;

When He yearns with all His heart

To create so great and bold a man

That all the world shall be amazed,

Watch His methods, watch His ways!

How He ruthlessly perfects

Whom He royally elects!

How He hammers him and hurts him,

And with mighty blows converts him

Into trial shapes of clay which

Only God understands;

While his tortured heart is crying

And he lifts beseeching hands!

How He bends but never breaks

When his good He undertakes;

How He uses whom He chooses,

And which every purpose fuses him;

By every act induces him

To try His splendor out-

God knows what He's about.

– Anonymous

Some "get it done" habits that are easy to learn begin with personal care and household chores. If we practice putting things back where they belong at home, it will become a habit, and we will automatically apply this habit everywhere we go. When you take out a stack of envelopes to pay the bills, return the unused envelopes to the drawer immediately. When you cut open a bag of chips with a pair of scissors, throw out the piece of cut wrapper right away and return the scissors to where they belong. When you make a habit of doing simple tasks like this immediately, there's nothing on the desk or counter nagging you to do a tiresome cleanup chore later. You're one step closer to preventing an out-of-control messy house.

Creative people can be messy — it is normal in the creative world to be messy. Still, it's not helpful to allow clutter to overtake our space and life. So, it's important to make it a habit to put things back where they belong after the project or job is complete.

Just before my twins were born, my house was neat and tidy. My closet was not as pretty as a retail store but organized enough that I could find matching clothes quickly. Then I went through a stage a year ago where I couldn't think straight. Every area of my life was filled with clutter. My head, my wardrobe, my office, my phone, my garage, emails, everything you can think of was in desperate need of an overhaul. All the clutter was causing unnecessary stress and added inefficiency that I couldn't afford in my busy daily life.

Taking responsibility for cleaning up after oneself will come in handy for every family member. When everyone pitches in to keep the house tidy and neat, we have a home that is comfortable and clutter free. Every family member benefits from the habit of cleaning up after themselves. Trash has a place. I call it the rubbish bin, you may call it the trash can. Whatever you call it, if you don't use it, you should start now! When we open up a package or remove a chocolate bar's wrapper, we should program into ourselves the habit of throwing the wrapper away immediately to avoid pests, melted chocolate all over the place or, worse still, a stain on our furniture that can never be cleaned up later.

Children are imitators; they do what we do. If mom and dad collect McDonalds trash bags in the car, their kids will grow up to do the same. Parents are busy, I totally understand. Still, at the end of my busy week, I constantly remind myself to throw away empty water bottles and all sorts of wrappers. When it's not a long busy week, I remind myself to do it daily or immediately. I haven't mastered what I am recommending, and I find it a daily struggle especially with hectic schedules. Still, clutter must be managed before it manages us.

> *I find clutter a daily struggle;*
>
> *Still, clutter must be managed before it manages us.*

Cleaning up and washing up are also important habits, because if these aren't just part of our routines, they can become painstaking tasks that get even more difficult because we dread them. Some people love washing dishes and some don't, but whether you like it or not, it has to be done. I know families who fight over washing dishes, laundry and cleaning up. Does that sound familiar? Believe me, we have all been there. Somebody has to do it! Try making these chores into habits, so they get done and are no longer a hassle. For goodness sake, be that somebody who doesn't make a fuss. There are charts created to help parents teach children age-appropriate chores. You can find them on Pinterest and many other online sites.[4]

Personal care, whether eating right, exercising, or getting to sleep early enough will make a big difference in our day-to-day lives once it has become a "get it done" habit. For instance, setting a time to sleep and sticking to the plan can be done easily once it's a habit. We will thank ourselves the next morning when we are ready to take on the day feeling fresh and happy. Our sleep and meals can affect our moods and our daily performance, so every little change we make will help.

"Get It Done" in Advance

Is your weekday as hectic as mine? There's always more to do, and even more that I want to do! One way I keep things a bit more under control is by setting myself up for success on Sunday night. I like to plan my outfits for the week if I have a busy week ahead that is filled with appointments and events. This habit helps me to know that everything is clean and ready to go. If I'm going to be away from the house during part of the day, I like to prepare some snacks or lunch basics for those days. Some parents like to do some dinner prep – maybe set up a crockpot for Monday night or chop and stash veggies for a few days worth of salads. Prepping helps especially when life throws unexpected events at us. When I make it a habit to get routine tasks done in advance, I have more bandwidth for the hectic surprises life always seems to have in store.

The World-Changing Power of Getting it Done

Like the saying "charity begins at home", the habits we learn at home will shape the way we do things in other parts of our life. These habits will allow us to move through basic tasks on autopilot wherever we go, reflecting a personality that is free to kindly consider the expectations and convenience of others. It's important to take care of public property the way we take care of our own homes. Putting shopping carts back in their place after shopping for groceries won't seem like a task because we are in the habit of putting things back in their places. If everyone cares to keep public restrooms clean and tidy, we all benefit from having comfortable restrooms. So this habit not only gets tasks done, it shows the world a person who cares about the needs of those around them.

Some of our habits can cause others irritation and problems. So we have to remember that our habits play a big role in not only our own lives but those of people around us. Being late for a meeting or event can cause irritation to those who put in the effort to be on time. I admit: this struggle can sometimes result from cultural differences that we need to be aware of and overcome. I remember taking the train back and forth from Milan, Italy to Lugano, Switzerland, a few years ago. My group missed our connecting train because of a delay, and when we approached counter agents in Switzerland for help rebooking, they said with irritation, "Of course it's delayed; it's coming from Italy."

I didn't quite understand the sarcasm, but a more experienced traveler in our group told us that the Italians are known for their extremely laid back attitudes and the Swiss are just the opposite. The Swiss despise tardiness. They take punctuality seriously and are always on time. As an Indian raised in Malaysia, punctuality isn't one of the cultural norms I grew up with. I am still struggling to master this habit, but believe me, it's necessary and makes a whole lot of difference in our relationships as well.

Get It Done Urgently: Time to Prioritize!

You might not think of setting priorities as a habit, but it's a challenging habit we all have to master. Sometimes we have several tasks in front of us, all of which seem equally important, but we can't do them all at the same time. Once, I had a screaming toddler, an emergency phone call and spilled coffee on the floor. I had to make quick decisions and prioritize: take the call, manage the spilled coffee and lastly handle the screaming toddler. It was hard to stay focused and attend to the call when my toddler was screaming for attention. I had to stand where the spilled coffee was so that nobody would slip and hurt themselves while I was answering the call. And if my toddler had been screaming due to a fall, my priorities would have been different. I would have attended to the child, the call and then the coffee.

Juggling priorities is something we have to master although it's challenging. Mastering the art of priority setting goes a long way when we need to decide which task to complete first.

The Gift to Children of Getting It Done

Children repeat what we say and will repeat what we do. Getting children to make their beds will help them embrace other significant habits in their lives. If I don't make my bed, how do I start teaching my child to do something I don't practice, you may ask. Well, it is never too late to adopt a new habit with your family. Do it for your child. Choose habits that will benefit them, and maybe get them Admiral McRaven's book as a gift[5]. A simple practice can change your life. After all, when you have set a tranquil and beautiful place for a good night's sleep, it is all worth it. Make your bed!

Habits to Practice

Maybe you don't think you're a very busy person. You don't have a long checklist of activities or a calendar with appointments and important errands for each day. Still, if you get into the habit of cleaning as you go, putting things away immediately, placing dirty laundry in the basket, sorting junk mail as you collect it and washing dishes after each meal, nothing piles up. If it does, don't beat yourself up. Just pick up and then return to practicing it as a habit. There is no greater feeling than the feeling of getting a task done.

Habits to Teach Children

When you sit down on Sunday night to make sure you're ready for the week ahead, gather the rest of the family to talk through what they need as well. It's best to ask children questions and allow them to get prepared for school rather than helping them pack their school bags. When we allow them to be accountable for their completed homework and preparation for school or their projects, we help them embrace the habit of getting the task done. This habit will serve them when life gets busier as they are older.

Chapter 3

Clean Up. Wash Up.

Little things add up, little efforts comfort, little lessons keep the calm,

Do you know that your hands need to feel the water filling your palm?

Feel the splash of those million drops of water, bouncing your cheeks and eyes!

Little teeth finding joy to smile as the toothbrush dances its steps on the rise!

Feel it, feel it all… breathe the air afresh and know there's joy…

In each and every faculties of your very self as you choose to employ –

-Them to… - Clean up. Wash up. Rise up and never give up or be shaken…

Little lessons keep you going strong. Little efforts shall energize you. Little steps are leaps taken.

Susan Ann Samuel

My grandmother and mother always managed to keep the house clean and were big into personal hygiene and cleanliness. Brushing teeth, showering, washing dishes, tidying, and keeping the house spotless—they would emphasize the importance of these habits all the time. It seemed normal to me to walk into a clean and spotless house. I used to think everyone lived that way. It was only when I became a young adult that I realized that some kids were raised by parents and grandparents who never practiced these habits.

I'm not saying that my mother and grandmother were perfect people. They had their own sets of good and bad habits just like all of us. However, I am thankful that they instilled this value in me because as a result, cleaning up after myself comes naturally. Washing dishes or keeping the house clean and tidy aren't a sweat . . . these come naturally because they're habits.

Now that I have children, I see the struggles people face with endless cleaning throughout the day. I am exhausted. It never ends. Sometimes I wonder how grandma and mom managed cleaning, cooking, and getting all the errands done. They made it seem so easy. It probably wasn't easy then either, but the difference was that they'd done these tasks repeatedly until they became habits. As I've mentioned before, habits help us function in autopilot mode. When we're doing something that has become a habit, it doesn't add stress or strain to us because our mind is programmed to carry out the task without dragging our feet. We just get it done.

Making a Habit of Cleanliness

Personal hygiene and cleanliness are essential habits. During the first two years of COVID-19, we saw and read about the importance of washing our hands and practicing personal hygiene almost everywhere. Who doesn't do this, I wondered. Surprisingly, many people need to be reminded to wash their hands often enough because it's not a habit for them. A simple habit of not washing hands can allow bacteria to grow, even to the point of causing terminal illness. This reason alone is enough for us to recognize the great importance of personal hygiene. In some Asian countries, people take a bath several times a day because of the humidity and weather which cause perspiration and uncomfortableness. Athletes in most countries do the same after their workouts. However, it becomes a habit not to shower frequently in countries where it's too cold or where people don't spend time doing activities where they sweat.

Why the Habit of Personal Care Matters

Personal hygiene, including dental care, cannot be taken lightly. Some infections are not within our control; however, we are able to avoid many health issues by cultivating and practicing good habits. Without proper personal care, tooth decay and diseases will creep up before we know it.

Why is it so important to emphasize personal hygiene? First, it is a foundation for good health. Physician-Scientist Dr. Sanya Thomas notes, "Maintaining proper personal hygiene is critical to preventing infectious diseases. Many infections spread due to poor hygiene practices, and preventive strategies can be learnt during these formative years. Additionally, it's important to keep your surroundings clean. This not only prevents transmission of diseases, but also helps you stay organized and focused."

It may surprise you how many medical conditions can result from poor personal hygiene. The pandemic has made us all aware that personal hygiene protects us against diseases, some of which can be serious or fatal. Poor hygiene also puts us at risk of skin rashes and fungal infections, body odor and smelly feet, fungal infections of the finger and toenails, and more. Good personal hygiene is important to staying healthy.

Just like every good habit, personal hygiene also adds value to our lives. I was amazed that one of my college business teachers assigned a book that taught personal hygiene. Until then, I thought this was something everyone automatically did, like putting on clothes before leaving the house. I guess it was good for college students to be taught that if they smell bad, they won't be liked at work and won't get promotions. Still, why would anyone need to learn this in college?

I actually told a classmate once that her body odor was pretty bad. I had to preplan how I was going to approach her because the last thing I ever wanted to do was offend her. I bought her a deodorant and asked casually if she used one. I suggested that she should start using one because it eliminates body odor, and that's how I had gotten rid of mine ever since I was a teenager.

Do you know that many people in some parts of the world consider deodorant a luxury item? This was one of my classmates in India, and I let her know that I understood that I was talking about something she might consider expensive. I did so by sharing with her about how I got my

Personal Hygiene Essentials

- Wash hands before and after eating
- Wash hands after using the restroom
- Take a shower after heavy exercise or sports practices
- Take a shower as we begin the day or before going to bed.
- Make the bed, change sheets weekly
- Use clean towels, dry towel after use
- Brush teeth daily, better yet twice a day

first deodorant as a gift from my aunt. The girl said she had seen deodorant in stores, but didn't know what it was for.

I had truly felt sorry for her when some kids laughed behind her back, so I'm glad I took the risk of speaking to her. She in return thanked me instead of shunning me or giving me a killer stare. Different people would react differently depending on their character, so think carefully before you do what I did. But you can definitely shower and save yourself from those disgusted faces!

So, wash up and clean up, and let your children learn from both your teaching and your example.

The pandemic reminded us that germs are everywhere, but we don't need a pandemic to wash our hands and keep clean. The US Centers for Disease Control says that simple hand washing with soap and water can reduce deaths from diarrhea-related diseases by almost half, and cut the risk of colds and other respiratory illnesses by up to twenty-one percent.[6] It will be too late if something bad happens to someone we love because of a bad habit. It's easy to make a good habit, and anything that becomes a habit is easier to do and follow.

Why the Habit of Tooth Care Matters

My grandmother cared for and raised my siblings and me when my mom started working. I love her dearly and miss her; she taught me many valuable life lessons that I hold close to my heart. I especially remember how long she spent each day carefully brushing her teeth.

"Ammama (grandma), why do you keep brushing your teeth for so long?" I would ask her in annoying tones, and she would respond with great energy that if I didn't take care of my teeth, I wouldn't have any when I get old.

"What!?" I'd exclaim. Nothing she said made sense to seven-year-old me. When Grandma was 84, her face was wrinkly and her body was frail. But her teeth were aligned properly, and they were sparkly white as snow. She had the prettiest smile.

Thanks to Grandma, my siblings and I brought home trophies and prizes for having clean teeth. Nurses would visit our schools from the dental clinics in Malaysia, and those of us with healthy sets of teeth would get awards to encourage hygiene. I wish this was still a practice. It was fun to receive new toothbrushes and attend dental hygiene workshops. The plastic skeletal model with teeth was my favorite part. The nurse had a humongous red toothbrush we could see even from the back of the classroom as she demonstrated how to properly brush and care for our gums and teeth.

Brushing teeth may feel like a chore if it doesn't become a habit. Once it is a habit, we don't spend much time thinking about it or have to make ourselves do it. Our hands automatically reach out to the toothbrush and toothpaste in the morning even with our eyes half open. We start the day by brushing our teeth. For others, the toothbrush comes out after coffee to avoid coffee breath. Whatever works for you, remember: it's a habit worth having so you'll have that beautiful set of teeth to smile with at your 84th birthday celebration. However, if children are not taught to make brushing teeth a habit, it can become a painful chore every single day.

We can start teaching our children to brush their teeth as soon as they can hold a toothbrush and have teeth. They don't all catch hold of the habit quickly. My toddler daughter loves brushing her teeth, but her twin brother loves to chew on his toothbrush. It will take a while for them to grasp the idea that it's important to brush their teeth. Making it fun with songs and having a routine helps them carry out this important habit daily.

Once again, proper dental care is crucial. Many people are not aware that poor dental hygiene can cause health problems. Health issues aside, I want you to have my grandma's smile at 84. Although my sweet grandma lost her battle to cancer, I will pass this habit down to my twins. I know grandma will be proud of me for practicing dental hygiene and all the other life lessons she taught me.

Please make a habit of brushing your teeth . . . at least the ones you want to keep.

Why the Habit of Home Care Matters

Our homes often reflect our personalities. Still, having a beautifully decorated home is not enough. Cleanliness and keeping it organized plays a big part in our daily life. I have friends who keep everything in their homes in order; I also know others who don't pay much attention to cleanliness and order. It's good to maintain a balance between being compulsive about cleaning and letting the house go until tidying up becomes a big project.

Have you watched the TV show Hoarders? Some of these families suffer from mental illnesses and depression. They've been filling the void in their emotional lives with things. Sadly, just clearing out the mess isn't a long-term solution for them. However, other people live overwhelmed with stuff because they just don't have the habit of cleaning or putting things back in place. Their chaotic spaces lead to depression and stress.

Why is home care an important habit?

First, home is where you live to unwind and spend quality time in your day. A clean and organized home will not only save you time when you are looking for something, but it will also give you a happy and peaceful feeling. An unclean house with crumbs and dust invites all types of bugs and pests. Overflowing trash cans will give an unpleasant odor and worse still, dust mites, bed bugs and germs can cause allergies, trigger breathing problems, and lead to diseases.

Secondly, if you are renting an apartment or a house, there are rules you have to comply with or you will be asked to vacate. In the "Hoarders" TV show, some people begin to take cleanliness seriously only after they receive a warning notice to vacate from the HOA or are warned by animal protection or child protective services that their pets or children will be removed from an unhealthy environment.

Thirdly, your children are watching you. They are going to follow your habits, so you want to model good habits for them to follow. Children learn how to cook, clean, and do basic chores from you. They won't know how to survive adulthood if you don't teach them these basic habits.

Clean and tidy up every chance you get, because house work is never ending. The only way to get things done is to keep doing a little at a time until it becomes a habit.

What Will Your Children Learn at Home?

I visited a friend and we sat down for dinner. After our casual chat and meal together, she had to leave for work. Her husband and two teenage sons began loading the dishwasher and cleaning up the table while the rest of us were still sharing conversations. Although we offered to help clean up, they politely declined and said they had it under control.

I was so impressed because I didn't see Mama asking her sons to help or even hinting at it with eye contact. She just kissed her boys goodbye. Cleaning up after dinner was so habitual a practice that they could keep doing the chores while holding conversations with the rest of us.

In another home, a mom proudly told me: "Oh, I pick up after my kids, they are princesses." Now, it's true that our children will always be our princes and princesses, but most of us are not raising the kind of royalty who have maids and bodyguards. We need to teach them to get used to chores because whether they like it or not, they will probably have to handle them for the rest of their lives. Even if you have hired help, you still are responsible for managing your home.

I can only hope that my twins will be as helpful as my first friend's teenage boys. But we all know that children have a mind of their own when they become teenagers. Some of them, all of a sudden, become "much older and smarter" than all of us. It can be unpredictable. Nonetheless, it's our duty as parents to teach them and help them establish good habits no matter how challenging it gets. Let your children hate you for a while, they will thank you someday even if they don't say it out loud. These life skills will add value to their homes someday, even when you are long gone.

Habits to Practice

Wash up and clean up daily. Personal care includes brushing teeth, showering, washing hands before and after meals and after using the restroom. Home care basics include placing dirty clothes in the laundry basket, washing dirty dishes, throwing trash into bins, cleaning up the fridge weekly before trash pick up day, cleaning paper clutter

IMPORTANT HOME CARE HABITS TO PRACTICE

- Put dirty clothes in the laundry basket
- Wash and fold the laundry
- Wash dishes after use or by the end of the day
- Clean the kitchen after cooking
- Clean and tidy up as you go.
- Put it away when you're done.
- Clean up the fridge and throw away old food
- Throw the trash into bins

daily once mail is picked up. These habits become easier when they become routine.

We must understand that children mirror us. We cannot teach them something we are not willing to do ourselves. So allowing them to watch us brush our teeth or showing them how to throw a candy wrapper in the trash can will help them imitate us. Maybe that's why it's said that children sometimes teach us more than we teach them.

As we get older, some of us realize that it's about time we change for the better to be good role models for our children. I personally know many people who dropped bad habits so that they could be good examples for their children.

Habits to Teach Children

Children are imitators, they do what we do. So remember that we have to do what we teach them if we want to effectively help them. They understand from seeing us that showering is a routine habit and brushing teeth is done daily. Everything we do daily is what we teach and guide them to do. Get them to throw trash into trash

> *Children mirror us. We cannot teach them something we are not willing to do ourselves. Maybe that's why it's said that children sometimes teach us more than we teach them.*

cans as soon as you open a gift or a candy bar, remind them to wash their hands after using the restroom, and explain to them why it's important. Get children to participate and do chores together during the weekend or small tasks daily to help them get into the habit of cleaning up. Play a fun song while getting chores done, make it a family event. Repetition is key when it comes to teaching children, and things like, cleaning up after themselves will come naturally as they grow older if they have been taught well when they are young.

Chapter 4

Please. Thank You.
I'm Sorry.
Excuse Me.

With the fire in every expressed word, you can batter or build,

You're born with the power to make change in this World, Oh Potter's Child,

So wield it… wield it in all goodness and mercy of the passion The Potter has skilled

In you. You, in your hills and valleys, can make beauty rise from the ashes, with every manner mild!

Reconcile, say you're sorry! Be grateful, say thank you! Be polite, say please and excuse me…

You won't lose anything! Let your words convey meaning!

With the fire in every enunciated word, there are battles to be won and these

Small soft spoken songs of Heaven's wisdom, will wield change and bring healing!

Susan Ann Samuel

Good manners set you apart because when you practice good manners, you make people feel comfortable and show them respect. Love and respect are the most important factors in any relationship. Whether you are at home, in school or work, having good manners shows that you care about the person you are around. It also takes humility and courage to say "I am sorry" when we have done someone wrong. Good habits can amend and heal relationships.

"Manners maketh a man." We live in a world full of people, we don't live on an island all by ourselves, so we must take into consideration the comfort and respect for people around us and not just focus on ourselves. The foundation of courtesy lies in good habits.

Why Manners Matter

Our good manners reflect in our everyday habits wherever we go. What we say, how we say, the way we talk, show respect and open doors for people throughout the day automatically

> *The habit of good manners can amend and heal relationships.*

become our character. If we don't pay enough attention or hold importance to practicing good manners throughout the day. It's easy to start and end the day by walking in a "bubble of rudeness" without realizing it.

Have you noticed that people who are likable have good manners and habits compared to those who are disliked? In order to make friends, we have to be considerate and respect each other. Manners and good ethics are principles that contribute to good friendships and relationships.

Imagine someone walking straight into you in their rush to get where they're going through a crowded place. If they don't say, "Excuse me," wouldn't that cause an unnecessary squabble? At work, customer service and respect for our clients and customers is a reflection of our professionalism and the importance we give our customers. Manners matter in business because customers who pay for services expect to be respected and want value in their services. However, many people who hold job positions take this lightly. Whether you are an employee or employer, talking to each other within your organization with respect is important and a wonderful culture to have.

When people don't bother with good manners, it can cause chaos in relationships everywhere we go. Have you heard people talking on the phone with their speakers on in a grocery store or listening to loud music in a public space. I always wondered if anyone took the trouble to teach them how to be considerate when they were children. Why are they oblivious that the rest of us are not interested in their conversation or their taste in music? I have seen two people argue with each other on public transport because one person had loud music on and didn't care to respect the solitude of other passengers. These disputes are unnecessary, but I have to applaud the person who had courage to politely attempt to put some sense into the inconsiderate person.

"Having these simple manners engraved in your daily living [nurtures] you into a kind and graceful human being who would become a strong team player in future endeavors," observes Physician-Scientist Dr. Sanya Thomas. "Irrespective of the profession you choose to pursue, this rare quality would prove to be highly valuable as you work with others on a day-to-day basis."

Four Basic Habits of Good Manners— "Magic Words"

Manners are habits, like so many other worthwhile things. Julian Baggini, writing in *The Guardian,* notes: "If we want to be good, we have to get into the habit of being good. And habits are formed by constant repetition of behaviors."[7]

Four small phrases form the foundation of a habit of good manners:

1. "Please" when you make a request
2. "Thank you" for what others do or give
3. "I'm sorry" when you're wrong
4. "Excuse me" when you interfere

Please

Oh please, say "please" when you are asking for something. If you don't, you sound like you are demanding.

This habit doesn't come easily to me. I actually have enough of a problem with this habit that I almost forgot to write about it. I am a big believer in good manners, and yet just like everybody, I struggle with a few myself. When I am asking for something, I will say, "Can you pass me the ketchup... please?" I know I am supposed to say please to be polite, but it just doesn't come naturally to me, so it doesn't make it to the beginning of the sentence. The only reason that I manage to add it at the end of the sentence is because I am constantly evaluating my own habits.

So, please remember that please is pleasant to the ears. Everyone around you will be so pleased when you ask them something beginning with "please."

Thank You

"Thank you" is a magic phrase that adds value to every relationship. I used to be upset when people didn't say thank you, then got used to it when I realized that the omission has become a norm. Young and old adults alike seem to lack the habit of thanking others.

An old fashioned way to express gratitude is by writing thank you cards. I admire people who take the time to do this. It is such a beautiful gesture, but only possible when we take time to prioritize this effort. I find it difficult to make that much time. But a text, a phone call, spoken words … I easily make time for these.

However we express our thanks, these two powerful words of appreciation warm both the recipient's and the giver's hearts. Using this phrase says a lot about you and how grateful you are. Your gratitude is a gift that keeps giving, and is also a powerful magnet that keeps you receiving reasons for more gratitude.

While you're expressing thanks to the people around you, remember also to be thankful for the many other things you enjoy in life. These can be entirely different for different people. A farmer might be grateful for rain; a tourist for sunny skies. Some are grateful for flowers in bloom, some for a quiet day fishing, others for an exciting ride on a motorcycle. You might follow the example of my pastor's wife (Trinity Church Dallas), who keeps a "grateful jar" that she fills with notes about everything she is thankful for. It's such a beautiful way to remind us to be thankful each day, prompting us toward a regular habit of expressing thankfulness to those around us.

I Am Sorry

"I am sorry" means apologizing for the mistake I have made and promising not to do it again, acknowledging how much it hurt the other person. Saying "I am sorry" helps heal relationships. Although it takes time to rebuild relationships, simply expressing our regret helps restore people's comfort with each other, because it demonstrates that both parties give importance to the relationship.

Some people hurt others intentionally, and some do it without realizing that they have caused someone injury. We should apologize as soon as we know that our deeds or words have caused someone hurt. Apologizing restores the relationship and gives peace to both parties involved.

I have been in situations where saying "I am sorry" restored a relationship that was affected by misunderstanding and miscommunication. On the other hand, I have also experienced situations where I had to set boundaries because I was repeatedly hurt by people who were not sorry for their actions and were not willing to apologize for their hurtful actions. It takes great understanding and wisdom to make decisions when someone has wronged us. We should learn to apologize if saying "I am sorry" is not a habit we are used to.

Excuse Me

We say "excuse me" for several reasons. It is the phrase we use when we ask someone else to give way to us, like when we are moving through a crowded room, or when we are asking them to give their attention to our immediate needs. We use it as an apology when we've done something embarrassing, like burp loudly, We also say "excuse me" to ask people to repeat themselves when we didn't hear them, or to let them know we need to leave the room[8]. In some countries, they say "pardon me" which has the same meaning. However you say it, it's a polite habit to practice.

Habits to Practice

As adults, we have to get into the habit of saying these simple phrases first if we want our children to learn them. Manners should be part of us and our way of life so that our children learn them with ease. Be considerate of others wherever you are, whether you are driving, walking or shopping. Holding doors for others and smiling are habits that can make a difference in someone else's day. Apply the golden rule: "Do unto others as you would wish them to do unto you." Be polite by paying full attention to those you are spending time with, and excuse yourself if you have to take a phone call or reply to a text message during your appointment. Watch your relationships and friendships blossom to strong bonds as you make a habit of using these four simple phrases.

Habits to Teach Children

Remind your children consistently to thank someone when they receive something even if they are teenagers and ought to know by now. Parents usually remind their toddlers to say thank you but for some reason they stop reminding their teenage kids. Don't forget that children watch you, so if you don't have manners, they never will practice good manners with ease.

Ask your children questions: How were they kind to someone today? Encourage them to spread kindness and instill good manners in them. Buy them books and materials that will help them develop good habits. Teach them table manners and appropriate etiquette both at home and if you eat out. When you are sharing space or a vehicle with someone else, remind children to always be courteous and respectful of others. We have to keep training children until good manners become a habit for them.

Chapter 5

Money Matters

Life is not a transaction, it is patience at every bone and marrow of action,

Called to be stewards of every ignited gift inscribed in our veins,

We are redefining laws of natural existence, we're adding grace to every reaction!

Meekly counting the little entrusted, to make it big… a business of eternal gains!

Life is not an illusion, it is trust and truth gliding at every impulse of the nerve,

Packed with so much potential, the Potter's Child needs to be tamed,

Shrewd at every move, loving at every moment, tracing an upward curve…

For an eternal pursuit, an undying passion so hopefully aimed

At one goal… Love! All what is invested in Love will be multiplied thousand folds,

This is a practice of habits, of a profitable pace, and of precision beyond our skill,

Money matters. Mindset matters. Miracles shall meet the shores of mercy as life at every second unfolds,

This is life. This is will. This is how we need to skill!

Susan Ann Samuel

Watching my parents manage money taught me life lessons: the do's and don'ts, the good and bad habits. My dad was a giver. I loved his generous heart and his good habit of giving, but I didn't like the way he lived as if there was no tomorrow. He never saved a dime; he just didn't know how to. My dad's bad habit of spending every penny he had and not saving up led us into many debts as a family. There were times when we were struggling for food and money to pay bills. He had a generous heart, but it wasn't enough to pay bills when bills were due.

My mom is also a giver, but she always kept enough for us before she gave away the extra. My parents separated when I was 11, and thanks to my mother's wise financial management we began to live a comfortable and secure life. She started working and taught me, by her words and especially by her example, how to save up and meet my financial goals.

7 Financial Habits I Learned from My Mom

From watching how my mom managed money as a single parent, I learned seven basic lessons about money that started me on a path to financial wisdom.

Pay your bills first.

This would seem to go without saying, right? But not everyone does. My dad loved making gifts and didn't always think first about whether the bills had been paid. That caused needless hardship, and in the end, I do believe that his bad money management habits caused the strain in my parents' relationship. Money problems are neck and neck with infidelity as the two top causes of divorce in the US today.[9]

The basics in my home growing up were paying bills and buying food. The basics in my home right now include maintaining a yard, budget for children and much more. Although the basics in life change, the habit of paying for the basics remains the same. Our children will probably be irritated and annoyed as we drill these important life lessons into them, because it takes effort and time to instill good habits in children. Our children learn best when we possess good habits ourselves, because then they can follow our steps and mirror us as they grow instead of simply

7 FINANCIAL HABITS I LEARNED FROM MY MOM

1. Pay your bills first, including church donations and tithes.
2. Save something, even if it's a small amount.
3. Achieve one financial goal at a time.
4. Pitch in - it makes a difference.
5. Budget for special occasions.
6. Avoid debt.
7. Work hard – work extra if you need to.

listening to our stories about the past.

Save something, even if it's only a small amount.

Early in my marriage, every time we had savings, something always came up and we'd use them. But that's not a bad thing. If we hadn't had any savings, we'd have gone into debt. We needed these small savings to replace worn car tires, repair an appliance, or meet some other unplanned need.

> *Mom always saved. She had a plan for what was needed next and a vision for the big picture.*

Money for emergencies is the first kind of savings everyone needs. It doesn't have to be a lot. This is money you save knowing that you will need to use it someday. You'll refill and empty this fund over and over. These are the savings that keep you from going into debt when a crisis hits.

When you're able to save more, you can also set money aside for other things. Those could include things like buying a new car or going on a vacation that you'd enjoy soon, or paying for a child's education or your own retirement. Sometimes you might decide that it's worth getting a second job or a side job to make saving possible.

We managed a Disney trip with relatives on a very tight budget because we knew our kids (nieces and nephews) wouldn't be kids forever. My husband worked a second job to help cover the costs. Those children are young adults now, and we're glad we worked hard so we could play hard with our families together. Some families spend years saving up for lavish weddings, there's nothing wrong in saving up for a lavish wedding, but remember to spend money where you make many lifelong memories together as well. Be frugal, not stingy when you decide to do something together with your family. It will always be worth it! Whatever you do, don't run into debt to impress others.

Achieve one financial goal at a time.

After my parents separated, my mother, my siblings and I moved into a rental house that was completely empty. No furniture. No appliances. No curtains. There were windows in every room, but they were hidden behind big plantation shutters that kept the house dark. We had no curtains, and curtains were not cheap. So for the first few months, we never opened the shutters. The house stayed dark throughout all day.

When mom finally saved up enough money for curtains, we were able to open up all the shutters one fine day and, finally, enjoy the glare of sunlight coming through the sheer sheets. I remember feeling the joy of just being able to draw the curtains to look out. Curtains were a big deal to us then.

Mom bought furniture and appliances one by one, saving up first and then making each purchase after she had enough money. She always had a plan for what was next and a vision for the big picture. Within a year, we had all the basic necessities. It felt like a big accomplishment to have a home with the basics. Our meals were simple but we had food, our bills were paid on time, and for the first time in a long time, I began to experience peace. The financial strain was gone.

Pitch in; it makes a difference.

In Malaysia where we lived, our basic expenses included school fees for books, materials, uniforms and more for my sister and me. By the time we were teens, we realized that mom's income couldn't cover everything. When I was 13 and my sister was 15, we approached a tourist gift shop owner asking for a job. I told the owner that we wanted to help our mother pay bills. I remember him asking me if I could smile and sell souvenirs to the tourists who were dropped off by tourist buses and vans throughout the day. I smiled wide and said, "Yes, I can do that!"

The store owner looked stern, but he was kind. I believe he hired me and my sister more to help us out than because he needed help. I will always be grateful for that job. It was fun watching Japanese tourists who wore big hats walk into the store in groups. I can't remember how many souvenirs I helped sell, but I do remember dreaming of someday touring another country with a big hat on.

My sister and I earned less than $100 a month from that souvenir store, but we also spent a few hours almost every day teaching English to children in our neighborhood. That brought in an additional $20 to help mom. These jobs taught us a great deal about budgeting at a young age. We need our children to get into the habit of pitching in for gifts, bills, and other financial decisions we make as a family. Pitching in teaches a great deal of responsibility.

Budget for special occasions

My mom worked extra hours whenever we had holidays coming. That's how we were able to have a Christmas tree and a good meal on Christmas day. We never ate out or spent money buying stuff unless we needed to. Mom taught us the difference between "need" and "want" at a young age.

Those lessons really helped me when I was older. I knew that sometimes the dollar budget for a special occasion might be very small, but I could use my ingenuity to make the occasion special anyway.

My husband and I spent $6,000 on our wedding at a time when a national survey showed that the average wedding cost more than $26,000.[10] We still wear the $90 wedding bands that we purchased at Walmart. My wedding gown rental was $50; his tuxedo cost $20. We bought a printer so that we could print our own invitations, food menu, wedding day itinerary, and more. We're just as married, and the pictures show just as much joy among the gathered friends and family.

When my mom visited us in America twelve years ago, my husband was a medical resident, and I was working part time in a legal office. We had very little income. We didn't have a lot to spend, so I showed my mom the town from a trolley (free to ride) that stopped at the art museum (free admission). We walked from another trolley stop to a reasonably priced restaurant for lunch before we hopped back onto the trolley to head home. We spent an evening walking along the Katy Trail, a miles-long path for walkers, runners, and cyclists in downtown Dallas. Enjoying simple pleasures that never involved much money, we were still able to make many memories and take tons of pictures.

Mom visited a few years ago and things were different. We could take her to a couple of fancy places to eat and treat her. That reminded me that good money management habits will help us to adjust and do what's necessary as our circumstances change. They help form a mindset in us, so we're ready to do with or without and to live the best way we can with what we have.

Avoid debt

You can tell that money was very tight during my childhood. In spite of that, mom refused to go into debt. She'd save up for what we needed, then purchase it. That meant it took a year to get all the appliances and basic furnishings for our rented house, but she never had to worry about getting behind on payments and having things repossessed. Once something was in our home, it was ours.

Later on, whenever my husband and I bought furniture or other large items on installment plans, I couldn't forget mom's reminders to pay off the debts. It was annoying, to be honest, but looking back I realize that those reminders formed in us significant habits that contributed to our skill in managing money wisely.

Work hard–work extra if you need to

My mom was a hard worker, and she was willing to work even more for something of value.

I remember the year my sister and I were elected to be school prefects. Prefects in Malaysia are students elected as "School Police" who help maintain order. Prefects maintain lists of the kids who break rules and have the authority to tell the chatty ones to be quiet. (I am pretty sure that I was elected because I was one of the noisy ones in my class – the teacher probably hoped the responsibility would help me become more serious.)

Prefects wore special uniforms that included a coat and matching pencil skirt, a blouse and a necktie. My uniform was maroon and my sister's was blue since she attended a different school. We would have to buy three sets of uniforms each, which would be tailored to fit us. All we needed was mom's signature on the approval form, and enough money to pay for the uniforms.

When we read the form to our mom, our excitement began to fade. We could tell that it was too expensive, especially since both of us had been elected the same semester and we would have to pay for six uniforms at once. It would be impossible for my mom to cover those costs. We were ready to let the opportunity go, but mom said, "You were both elected and I am so proud of you, so I am going to work extra hours to get you your uniforms."

I remember asking: "Are you sure, mom? It's okay if we don't accept it." We were willing to pass on the opportunity, but my mom managed to pay for our uniforms by working extra and using some of her savings. That alone taught me the importance of saving and working a little extra to achieve a goal.

Lessons I Practice as an Adult

The lessons I observed in both my parents' lives have helped shape my own approach to money in our family. Here are several.

Live Within Your Means

While my husband was still studying, we had to live very carefully. We lived in an apartment. Our fridge leaked and our one car with its clunking and squealing noises sounded like it was falling apart. We couldn't afford a washer or dryer, so all week I collected the quarters I got in change, then walked with my whole load of laundry and a heavy bottle of detergent to the laundromat at the end of the

> *You don't need to follow trends and impress others. What's most important is to build good credit and make wise decisions for you and your family.*

block. I had to wait there through the wash and dry cycles, because people were quick to steal clothes from unattended machines.

There are always silver linings in difficult times, of course. I got a lot of reading done while I watched my loads cycling. I met many different people at the laundromat and exchanged interesting conversations with my neighbors. Still, I'm glad we now have the means to own a washer and dryer in our own home.

Living according to your means comes down to one simple resolve: Whether you have little or more, make the most of it. During those student days, we equipped our apartment with furniture, decorations and appliances we purchased from Craigslist and the Salvation Army store. I remember the excitement of our newlywed "date nights" when we'd walk to Little Caesars Pizza, spend less than $10 for a pizza, drinks and cheese sticks, then spend a whole extra dollar to rent a DVD for a movie night at home.

Tight finances often meant inconvenience. Since we could afford only one car, my husband would drop me off at college on his way to the hospital. My classes started at 8 am, but he had to drop me off at 6:30 am if he was to arrive on time, so I would settle in on a bench outside the library, which didn't open for another hour. He also couldn't pick me up until 8:30 pm. It didn't take long for campus security to realize I wasn't a threat and even, quite kindly, to let me into the library a half hour before it opened. The library was my favorite place to study and hang out, and with our shared car shaping our schedules, I did a lot of studying and hanging out there.

I can go on and on about how being frugal helped us make the best of what we had then. We do splurge these days if we want to, however, our habits of saving and living with less allow us to give to others, donate, invest and own businesses. Habits play a crucial role in all our decision making.

Give Generously and Wisely

My dad was a giver, and I know that I learned this beautiful habit from him. He didn't take a second to think before giving. As a result of watching him, giving came naturally to me starting when I was very young. It was easy for me to give away my candy or anything extra.

That said, my father made many bad financial choices, and his life lessons and experiences have taught me to be wise in giving. My favorite book, the Bible talks about giving and I use it as a compass. The Bible talks about learning from ants that save up food in summer for cold winter days (Proverbs 6:6-8). It also mentions that God gives to us according to the same scale we use when giving to others (Luke 6:38). The lessons I apply from the Bible are proven to work.

Growing up as the child of a single mother in Malaysia, mom tried to make sure that we had what we needed, but we didn't always have what we wanted. It took a lot of creativity on our part and sometimes generosity on the part of others to make even life essentials available. I've already told you in chapter 1 (Testimony-Not Green Lentils) about the time a teenage friend heard me say that we were hungry, and she got her father to help her bring us food. We didn't have enough, and they had more than enough. So they used their abundance to make sure we had what we needed. God promises to provide enough for us all, and also says that one way He provides for us is through the excess of others. When we know we have everything we need and also many things we want, then it's easy to realize that we can give generously to help others.

As Christians, our family makes it a habit to give 10 percent to the church, because we see the church as the place that helps people with every kind of need. So, if we get paid or receive $100 as a gift, we give $10 to church.[11]

You don't have to be a Christian to apply this method of giving. You can give 10 percent in other ways. Maybe you want to help provide food for hungry children in the US, or supply chickens to small farmers in other countries. You might want to invest in education, like Serbian tennis player Novak Djokovic, who has built fifty schools from his prize money.

You could give to help fund housing for homeless veterans or pure water supplies in rural communities overseas. The range of opportunities is endless, which makes it easy to pick a way to give that matters to you and your family.

Teaching children to give is crucial. Most children don't enjoy giving 10 percent away, and; even some adults struggle with this. What most people don't realize is that their giving doesn't just bless the people they assist, but that their own lives are blessed by giving. Try this and watch your remaining 90 percent grow. I have personally experienced this, and I cannot begin to describe it because it's almost magical.

Saving and Investing

The habit of saving and investing will add peace of mind to you in the long run. Saving money requires discipline and wisdom. Have you heard of impulse buying? Some people spend money on clothes they never use because they spend unnecessarily while window shopping in a mall. One of the biggest mistakes I used to make in my early twenties was to go window shopping with my friends all the time. I learned that I could control my spending if I stayed at

> *The best investment you can make is to first teach yourself lessons you never learned.*

home. It's almost the same with eating, if you don't have a bag of chips in your pantry, you most likely won't eat any. When you know your bad habits and begin to acknowledge them, it is easier to tame the questionable actions that get in your way.

Some habits start with a mental decision. My goal to save up money for a house downpayment motivated me to end habitual spending for unnecessary "wants." When I only spent for my needs, I was able to save enough to achieve my goals. I set a budget and achieved it by sacrificing meals out and trendy clothes. I never thought it was possible because I knew I had some bad habits that had a pretty stronghold on me. However, I won the battle in my mind. And with discipline, I managed to buy my first house when I was 26 with savings from money I earned myself. After that achievement, I realized that if I applied the habit of saving and budgeting, I could achieve anything I wanted.

It took me years to save up for that first house, so we must remember that we have to be prepared to practice certain good habits for a long time to achieve something in life. The good thing about habits that benefit us is how natural they can become, allowing us to use them over and over while knowing they work for the best.

If your money disappears before your next paycheck, it's hard to think about saving and investing. Life happens and the next need or newest trend will steal all your money before you blink your eyes. It's important to be wise like an ant and save up for the rainy day. This Bible verse is a great reminder to prepare for uncertain circumstances: "Go to the ant, O sluggard; consider her ways, and be wise.

Without having any chief, officer, or ruler, she prepares her bread in summer and gathers her food in harvest" (Proverbs 6:6-8 ESV).

Life happens, so we ought to prepare for the challenging times that inevitably come.

Saving vs. Investing: What's the Difference?

It's important to understand the difference between saving and investing. Saving comes first. You save for immediate needs, like when my mom saved to buy each piece of furniture for our empty rented house. You save so you can cover needs you can foresee that might land at unpredictable times, like the expensive car repairs that start to hit after the first 100,000 miles or so. You might be ready to save for a child's education or your own retirement. Money that you save is kept where you know it's safe and where you can easily get it when needed. For most people, this will be a savings or checking account. Longer term savings, like for college or retirement, usually are put into special kinds of accounts.

Once you're in the habit of saving and have enough money put aside to meet your foreseeable needs, you will be more prepared to start investing. Investing involves risk. When you invest, you take a chance that you may lose the invested money, or if you're fortunate, gain more from the investment.

Have you heard the saying, "Don't put all your eggs in one basket"? This quote simply means when you put all your efforts toward one thing, you will lose it all if you lose. In an investment context, if you have saved up some money and you are ready to invest, it's wise to put a fraction of your savings in investments instead of risking it all. Some investors will beg to differ as they have experienced the opposite outcome, having taken big chances and succeeded by putting all the eggs in one basket. But if taking big risks isn't one of your habits, investment isn't the place to try it first. If our habits that are driven by morals and principles bring us peace and success, we are doing something right. Why try something else if the first approach is working?

Whatever we do, making wise financial decisions is a habit we must apply and teach our children. Allowing children to make decisions about their finances will give them a better taste of reality than if parents back them up financially all the time. When you bail them out regularly, children develop the habit of taking excessive risk because they lose nothing and will not be impacted.

Teach your children the importance of saving and investing for the future instead of focusing on keeping up with all the latest gadgets and clothes. It's okay to like trendy fashion, just remember to set aside some money so that you don't spend it all on what you only want. Choosing between what you want and what you need will be a constant battle throughout life, and learning to make wise decisions can only be achieved through habits. I know the struggle because I am a fan of nice things, but you can have both if you master the art of saving and budgeting.

Pay Taxes, Gratuities and Interest Rates

Taxes and gratuities can come as a surprise when we pay for a purchase or a meal. Eventually, we learn that they are just a part of the price we'll pay. But for children, in particular, it helps to talk about these costs and what they mean.

A 10-year-old boy was elated when he received $100 for Christmas. He said, "Yay! I can buy the shoes I want! They're on sale for $99.99."

We all know what happened when he raced to the store. He found himself short, because he didn't know how to count the entire cost of his purchase. Local and state sales taxes could increase the price by $7.50 or more. He would have been disappointed that he didn't have enough money in his pocket.

The same thing often happens to teenagers when they want to buy their first car. The car they can afford, based on their savings, may cost much more than they can afford after figuring in the costs of gas, insurance, maintenance, and annual taxes and registration fees.

One author suggests using receipts to help children understand taxes. When you leave a store, point out the purchase price and the sales tax numbers on the receipt. Explain that the sales tax goes to communities to buy things we all use. It helps pay for playgrounds, schools, fire trucks, libraries and police cars.[12] A small amount of sales tax money, collected from everyone every time they make a purchase, adds up to meet big community needs.

In the same way, you can point out gratuities on a restaurant receipt. You can also let your children be the ones to place the gratuity on the table, in a servers' tip jar or into the hotel housekeeper's envelope, to help them form the habit of generosity toward those who serve them.

Interest rates are almost like thieves eating into your funds if you overlook this important factor when budgeting. Get into the habit of paying off debts and loans with higher interest rates first. Avoid using credit cards if you haven't mastered budgeting habits. This will save you from the interest rate trap that you can get tangled in if you are not careful.

When children are old enough to hold a "real" job, remind them that their more grownup job comes with new grownup responsibilities. They will be paying income taxes, just like you do, and some of these will be deducted in advance from their paycheck. That way, they won't face the "sticker shock" of a paycheck that is less than expected.

A good lesson plan about taxes for children is found on a U.S. government website.[13] It covers:

- What taxes are, who pays taxes and why we pay them

- The general concept of taxes, why they exist, and how they work

- Different type of taxes

- Some goods and services that are paid for with taxes

- The basic process of collecting taxes

Let's focus on teaching and implementing these habits of calculating tax, interest rates and gratuity, so that both children and adults won't forget to add those important numbers to their next purchase.

Habits to Practice

Giving/tithing, paying bills, saving and investing: keeping these all in focus is a proven formula to successfully handle money. If your bills are higher than your wages, you probably need two jobs. If you know the difference between wants and needs, you will probably be able to start saving money. If you never had a good role model who managed finances wisely, pick up a good book and start teaching yourself about saving and investing.

The best investment you can make is to first teach yourself lessons you never learned. When you have little money, live like a minimalist, if you have more money, live like a minimalist as well, but don't forget to treat yourself. You don't need to follow trends and impress anyone but yourself because what's most important is to build good credit and make wise decisions for you and your children. Teach your child to fish instead of giving him a fish. Let children manage their finances, teach and guide them, reward them when they have mastered good financial habits. I love this nugget of wisdom from the Good Book which goes, "An inheritance obtained too early in life is not a blessing in the end."(Proverbs 20:21) If we pay all our bills, pay our tithes or donations, save some money and keep learning ways to make good financial decisions, we will be able to pass on to our children these valuable lessons.

Habits to Teach Children

Responsible handling of money can be taught to young children through leading by example, Physician-Scientist Dr. Sanya Thomas notes. Simple strategies, such as transferring a percentage of your paycheck into your savings account or creating daily and monthly budgets for expenses, demonstrate practices that will prove incredibly helpful when children leave the nest for college or work, she finds. It's also important to teach about responsible handling of credit cards and taking loans. Disciplining yourself in the use of these easily available resources will prevent you from falling into the debt trap many individuals fail to recover from, and it will also teach your children to avoid this risk, she notes.

One of the most important habits a child needs to learn is to give. As a child, I learned to give and this beautiful habit multiplies other goodnesses in unexpected ways. Giving, saving, budgeting and understanding the value of money are necessary life lessons and habits every child should be taught. Budgeting is a must!

We shouldn't spend money we don't have because sooner or later this habit will cause us inconveniences. Allow children to pitch in for bills at home once they start earning money, especially for those who are living with you. Teach children to save money to buy their siblings and friends gifts with their money. Pitch in to help them when they are short of money, but also teach them to budget and buy gifts they can afford. If they only have two dollars, take them to the dollar store to buy a gift, remind them to add tax to their purchases. It doesn't matter if your family is well off, if your child has $2 saved, that's all he can afford. Teach him or her about managing his or her money, you will be so proud of him or her someday.

Chapter 6

Work Hard. Play Harder

*Did someone tell you that there is a fallout at the end of
your trying?*

*That you couldn't do what you're born to do? That you
will never stop crying?*

*Turn your ears to the whispers of Love calling out to you.
Hear it above the noise…*

*Turn your heart to the wonder of a new start at every
second step. This is your choice!*

*Work hard. Play harder. See the way the cosmic will cheer
on your striving,*

*And how beyond the winning or the losing, your heart
will know the meaning,*

*Of the precious passion in you that will continue to
persuade you to give it all*

*Oh Potter's Child, keep running… you're born to win,
you're born to follow an eternal call!*

*So plant your dreams in the soil of hope. Water with your
sweat and tears,*

*Plant with love and a lot more love, and reap a harvest of
love that steers*

*The World to a better tomorrow, purer triumph,
tranquility…*

*This is your choice, your next step, your work, your play,
and your victory!*

Susan Ann Samuel

Serbian tennis pro Novak Djokovic started playing with a toy racket and a foam ball at age 4 and by age 35 he had broken record after record. His prize earnings of more than $158 million (USD) make him the all-time earnings leader in men's tennis.

Everyone enjoys winning. Winning gives children the chance to learn important lessons about hard work, teamwork, and the importance of competition. Losing teaches other lessons— about resilience, empathy, and accurate self-understanding. And whether a child is working hard to master a task or to master a game, they learn important life skills from working hard.
– Physician-Scientist Dr. Sanya Thomas

In 2008, the tennis world was marveling at how the 20-year-old Djokovic had crashed into the world of the greats. Others were marveling at how the young man was already investing in the success of children who had been consigned to society's "loser" pile. By the time he reached age 35, his Novak Djokovic Foundation for early childhood education had already constructed fifty schools.

It's also critical to maintain a healthy balance between working and relaxing, notes Physician-Scientist Dr. Sanya Thomas. You can get high quality work done and be highly productive if you schedule timely breaks to reflect and rejuvenate, she says. "Just as a machine needs to be regularly serviced with the highest quality materials, humans also need high quality rest to maximize their potential and be efficient in the work they do," Dr. Thomas reminds us. "Rest can be anything that brings you peace and joy personally, but hitting that pause button at the needed intervals will add a spring to your step as you walk the difficult path to achieving long-term success."

What Children Learn from Hard Work

"Teaching our little ones to persevere when things get tough and to work hard to achieve their goals and aspirations is one of the most important skills our children can learn," writes Mikelle Despain, a work-from-home single mother.[14] Psychologist Angela Duckworth has studied for many years what makes people successful in life. Perseverance – what she calls "grit" – and hard work turn out to be the keys.[15]

Despain suggests several strategies for developing the habit of hard work and perseverance in children:

Encourage them to try new things. New activities include new challenges. Encourage them to keep up the hard work, and help them find solutions when something isn't working out.

Praise them specifically. "Good job!" will never mean as much as "Wow! I'm so impressed that you're able to play your scales faster. You've been practicing a lot!"

Praise them for their hard work. Even when they haven't yet reached their goal, praise them for continuing to practice the skill.

Let them fail. It's okay not to succeed the first time. Sometimes you have to fail a lot of times before you figure out how to do something. Be patient! Show them you believe they'll be able to work it out.

Let them do the work. Coach them, sure; but don't do the job for them. When you take over, you teach them that they don't need to make the effort that success will require.

What Children Learn from Winning

The experience of winning helps children, Djokovic's foundation acknowledges: "Life is competitive, and children learn that it's best to be good at things from a young age."[16]

What else can children learn from winning?

Self-Confidence: Success produces confidence, and confidence in success encourages children to work hard. "The experience of winning helps children get motivated to take the next steps to achieve even bigger goals," the foundation notes. Those successes could be at school, in sports, in creative

174

activities, or any number of things.

Teamwork and Cooperation: Kenneth Barish, a professor of Psychology at Weill Cornell Medical College, points out that competitions of all kinds "can help parents teach their kids about the importance of teamwork, commitment to a task, cooperation and respect for the opponent." [17]

Strategy: When competition involves strategy, it helps children learn how to both follow the rules and find the most advantageous path for reaching their goals.

What Children Learn from Losing

As much as we all like to win, losing in childhood competition is also good practice in habits that fuel lifetime success.

Resilience: No one likes to think about losing or to see a child crushed by losing. But everyone wants their children to be resilient, and what's resilience but the ability to bounce back from a loss? An article from the Novak Djokovic

"By showing them that losing is not the end of the world, children learn that life is full of second chances."
- Anne Steinhoff Novak Djokovic Foundation

Foundation points out: "While it is important for parents to teach children to win and succeed, teaching them to lose is just as important. By showing them that losing is not the end of the world, children learn that life is full of second chances."[18]

Sense of Competence: When children rebound from a tough situation, they learn that they can deal with tough situations. This can reduce or prevent anxiety, because they learn from experience that a bad situation isn't the end of the road. They discover that it's possible to learn from mistakes, then get right back in the game.

Commitment to Hard Work: When we lose, we also can become more committed to the hard work it takes to do better next time.

Empathy: Experiencing disappointing losses also gives us more empathy for those who are sad and disappointed.

Self-Understanding: How many times has your child protested a loss by crying, "It isn't fair!" They're not usually protesting a bad call by a referee, they're complaining about how much easier the game seems to come to the child who won. In truth, life doesn't give everyone the same gifts. But life gives each of us the fair chance to do the most we can with the gifts we've been given.

It's Not Whether You Win or Lose: Sportsmanship

So we know it is important to work hard. We agree that we all learn lessons from both winning and losing. And one of the most important lessons to learn is that it's essential to treat well the people we meet as we compete and work hard. It's called good sportsmanship, and it matters in all of life. Many habits of good sportsmanship help us as adults, too:

- Make no excuses for failure. As the saying goes, "If you lose, don't make an excuse."

- Don't gloat in victory. "If you win, don't rub it in."

- Follow the coaches' directions, and accept the decisions of officials. No arguing!

- Encourage your teammates, even when they've let you down.

Good sportsmanship is a way we can show ourselves and others that we care more about our relationships than our achievements.

What Kids Learn from Playing

It's also important for kids to just play, without competing. Play has lots of benefits, but many kids don't get enough chances to enjoy them. Parents organize busy schedules of organized activities, so there's not much time for children to just play. Schools don't give much time for recess, and screen time is replacing play for even very small children. The average preschooler is onscreen 4.5 hours a day.[19]

Why does play matter? It seems so unorganized and purposeless. The experts say there's more to play than we might think.

Play builds friendship and relationship skills. It helps children learn to get along with others. They have to learn how to regulate their own emotions in the process, which is a very valuable life skill.

Play strengthens kids against stress. Play is a habit that relaxes, focuses and energizes. Playing with others is a habit that builds relationships. All of these are great stress busters and help push stress away. One study found that preschool children anxious about entering preschool became dramatically less stressed after fifteen minutes of play – and that stress levels dropped more in kids who played than in children who listened to a story.[20]

Play teaches planning and organization. When a child decides to put the toy pot on the toy stove before turning to care for a baby doll, that's planning. When a child discovers that the sand channel they've just dug brings a wave to wash away their castle, that leads to organizing the next dig – or filling in all the possible channels. These seemingly simple activities help children discover cause and effect, find out that they can influence their world, and practice for planning the steps to take toward their desired outcome.

Playing with children benefits adults, too. It's relaxing and fun – those are givens. But it also has health benefits that last for years. Did you know that adults who play with children burn 20 percent more calories a week than others? That playing with children in midlife makes you one-third less likely to get Alzheimers in your 70s? Playing with children helps in their development and your health – benefits for everyone![21]

Why Adults Need to Play

Children are so carefree and happy when they play. As we grow older, we forget to play or take a fun-filled break. Successful people know how to work hard and also to play hard, because incorporating play into our lives adds many wonderful memories and life experiences while recharging us to be more efficient and happier.

Play for adults isn't just activities that you schedule. It could be as simple as watching something funny and laughing. Taking laugh breaks is important! Sometimes I catch my husband chuckling away to some stand-up comedian or laughing out loud as he shares riddles back and forth with his nieces and brothers. Laughter is indeed the best medicine! Just like charging our phone batteries, breaks are essential for our mental health. Spend time outdoors, take walks, play a sport, dance to your favorite song or just cycle around.

I read for the first time about supernovas in one of my children's story books. A supernova is an explosion that happens within a massive star that causes it to die. I never knew that a star could get burnt out. It sounds pretty cool, but it also sounds kind of sad. It reminded me of the human stars that got burnt out from the stresses of their lives or the pressure of being a star. From movie stars to musicians and fashion designers, the list is sadly long. Did they forget to play and lighten up when days were rough? I always wondered what drove them to emotional breakdown. Could a simple habit of playing help ease the tension?

Stress is a common factor in our human lives. Whether you are a child, a student, a stay at home mom tending to a child or a CEO of a company managing hundreds, you will have to deal with some form of stress in life. A stay at home mom is a "star" in her family and she can get burnt out too.

Your child who is involved in many different co-curricular activities can also suffer burnout. I know a few unhappy people who are workaholics in their jobs. They feel guilty for taking a break from work and they sometimes don't know how to enjoy a vacation where you do nothing but have a good time.

Do you know what happens when we get burned out? We get irritated easily, lose sleep, get depressed, become ill and turn into a cranky person and that can ruin our relationships. Going on for a long duration of time without "play" or "breaks" won't help you emotionally, physically, or mentally. I love how Stephen R. Covey describes our need for work breaks in his book 7 Habits of Highly Effective People. He uses the metaphor of sharpening the saw you use to cut wood: If you never stop cutting, you get less and less done, but if you stop to sharpen your saw, you will complete the job more quickly and easily.

So, take a break, go on vacation, watch something funny or entertaining, eat that cake! You are more efficient when you stop for refreshment and sharpen the saw.

Habits to Practice

Hard work always pays off, and it allows us to sit back and enjoy the fruits of our labor. However, it is necessary to make a habit of living a balanced life. We can't have it all, yet

181

we can create a balanced life by carving out time to play every now and then. Play in this context simply means making time for leisure. But be sure to spend time with family and friends. Life is meaningless if all we possess are material things and accolades. The hard work we put in to raise our children will be more meaningful when it is filled with rich memories like playing in the playground, hiking, being outdoors, fishing or just gazing at the stars together. Life will always have it's highs and lows, "sometimes we win, sometimes we lose," but we learn from our experiences and keep moving on.

Habits to Teach Children

Teach children the value of hard work and its rewards, remind them that hard work involves sacrifices which will eventually pay off, but be certain they also learn to make fun activities one of the ways they reward themselves. Again, children learn best when you demonstrate how it is done. So perhaps plan a fun family activity to conclude a hard week of study. After end-of-term exams, do something special together. Whether you have little money or more to spend, there are many ways to have fun with your family. Numerous countries and cities offer events throughout the year that involve very little spending. Take time to do something fun so that everyone will be recharged for the next week's or next term's hard work. Create a routine that can build habits your child can carry into the future. Praise your children for the victories and encourage them to try harder when they lose. Remind them that it's important to always keep a sportmans spirit, accepting success with humility and failure with challenging efforts to do better.

Chapter 7

Building
Relationships

There is a sound of music touching notes of every syllable of love at every heartbeat,

There are moments when nothing seems to make sense, none seems to understand your call for the feat,

But the breath in you is not to defy the goodness or the light in yourself or others. They'll know

Yes! They will know that the passion you sow is that which will make a community grow.

So walk the extra mile, be kind, be caring and give clarity to what is blurred;

Set the trend of being preciously led by your conscience undeterred,

To build bridges, cherishing relations and encouraging pure passions,

So hear me, Potter's Child, pay close heed, Potter's Child – this is you, as you mold yourself in gracious compassion

Imaging the uneasy reality, orchestrating the effort that negates entropy.

Remember, your hope can make people have hope in themselves and it'll dare them to look and see

That life has its meaning when we are together, every human, every sister and every brother,

And the universe will sing along with us… a song of love, a song of power!

Susan Ann Samuel

Strong and lasting friendships and relationships are based on trust, good communication, support, honesty, respect, compromise, good boundaries, empathy, going the extra mile and spending time. It takes intentional love and effort to build relationships.

Two are better than one, because they have a good return for their work. If one falls down. her friend can help her up. Ecclesiastes 4:9-10 (paraphrased)

It's so important to have supportive friends and family! As the poet John Donne said, "No man is an island." We all depend on each other, which means everyone is important in some way to everyone else. Still, the people most important to us day-to-day will be those with common interests. Some will prove to be kindred spirits. Look for your tribe, and you will find them.

Genuine relationships become highly valuable when navigating life's hardest battles, Physician-Scientist Dr. Sanya Thomas says. "An important determinant of happiness when life gets busy or messy is the presence of high-quality relationships."

Home is the place where children begin learning how to build those relationships, she says. "The seeds to developing good, healthy relationships can be sowed in the fertile grounds of a young family's home. Children are keen observers, and even though parents may be unaware, children constantly observe what people in their surroundings do and then imbibe their qualities, good or bad," Therefore, Dr. Thomas finds, it's vital to set the kinds of examples for children that you wish to see them emulate in their adult lives as they grow and develop. As she puts it, "The subtle interactions between parents [and] other household members, interactions between older adults and children, and the values instilled in these impressionable minds and hearts shape the kind of adult a child would grow into."

That doesn't mean relationships are always easy. The Bible puts it this way: "Iron sharpens iron, and one man sharpens another" (Proverbs 27:17 ESV). No one tries to sharpen an iron tool with butter because the tool would slice through it. You sharpen an iron tool with something equally hard. You grind it against something that is equally durable yet different. Only in these types of relationships will we learn the habits of adapting, accepting, being flexible, understanding, and not being difficult.

The Qualities of a Friend

We trust our friends to live out several qualities over time, all of which make the relationship more valuable, encouraging, and nurturing to us both.

Communication

Good communication is a "must-have" habit in any form of relationship. I've heard a preacher speak about the "trust bank" that each one of us has. He used this theory to explain how relationships fall apart. Every good deed a person does, he explained, deposits trust into the bank of the friend. When things go wrong and tension arises in conversations or deeds, an amount of trust is withdrawn from the account. So, basically, the account has to be sound, with more deposits than withdrawals, to have a great bond with someone. [22]

If all you do is hurt, lie and break your promises, you keep withdrawing from your account. And if your bad habits weigh more than your good habits, your relationships are doomed. When you leave your trust bank empty, you will no longer have a relationship with someone.

I love this perspective because I believe in giving chances and giving people the benefit of the doubt - many times. Nonetheless, when a person disrespects and disregards boundaries over and over again, I would apply the "trust bank" theory. There is nothing left to withdraw from a one-sided relationship. Like the saying, "it takes two to tango" - you cannot build a relationship by contributing and depositing from someone who continually withdraws by being rude, irresponsible, disrespectful and mean. These are just examples of how certain characteristics that are formed by habits can be detrimental to forming long, strong relationships.

One of the most important ingredients in building friendships and relationships is being able to communicate effectively and with transparency. If you can communicate with someone and share your thoughts, expectations, frustrations and reasoning with them, and if they can do the same with you, even broken relationships can be restored. The only time communication does more harm than good is if you are communicating with someone who is in denial of their actions or someone who will not acknowledge that they were wrong, although clearly they were. In situations like this, I will no longer waste time communicating. A person who is not sorry for their actions and keeps repeating their poor actions is not worth communicating with, since they don't have the wisdom to comprehend what you are saying, or they simply don't have love and respect for you.

Words are powerful and so are actions. People sometimes communicate using different methods. If someone claims that they love you but their actions don't align with their words, it's clear that you don't really matter. If you are unsure, it's better to ask someone a question rather than assuming because sometimes we can misunderstand someone and get it all wrong.

Having said that, even the sweetest person can be disliked. As the saying goes, "You can be the ripest, juiciest peach in the world, and there's still going to be somebody who hates peaches" (Dita Von Teese). In this case, remember that your tribe are people who love peaches. Stick with them. Focus on the people who are with you now.

We lose friends throughout our lives, and people who are part of our life for just short periods are still valuable. Brian "Drew" Chalker wrote a beautiful poem about friendships that reminds us that some people are with us for a reason, some for a season, and some for a lifetime.[23] One friend might meet a specific need; engage with you in a particular season of growth; or remain with you through all your years. Friendships "for a reason" end when our need for them ends, even though they might end before we think we're ready. Friendships "for a season" allow us to learn, grow, and share, often with great joy. Still, they pass as this season of life ends. "Lifetime relationships," on the other hand, build the foundation of all our other relationships. They teach lessons in love that may come with great blessings and may come at great personal cost. All of these kinds of friendships are gifts for which we must give thanks.

Giving and Receiving

Friends both give and receive. Sometimes I'm filled to overflowing and live selfless from my abundance and sometimes I'm in need so I ask my friends for support. Sometimes I may be so needy as to appear selfish! Still, when my friends are hurt, I listen and encourage; when I'm hurt, I know they'll do the same. When they need something I have -- whether it's knowledge, the loan of a garden tool, or something else -- they know I'll share, and I know they'll share when I'm in need.

Exceeding Expectations

Friends go the extra mile for each other; exceeding expectations. Sometimes this seems small and simple. Even on a busy day, a friend might fit in a needed ride to the mechanic or the airport. Sometimes friendship requires more. We pull out the sofa bed or open the guest room to a friend who lands in town, buy groceries and do housework for the friend who's just had surgery.

Honesty and Integrity

Friends are honest with each other, and are able to tell the truth even when it's uncomfortable. For example, they will say why they won't be able to attend an event or be truthful about something concerning the other that might be helpful. Integrity involves applying good principles that represent who you are, despite what others believe.

Being Humble

Friends are humble. They don't lord it over each other; they celebrate with each other instead of demanding always to be the focus. If you're doing better, you don't rub it in. When they're doing better, you congratulate them. To be humble is not to make yourself small, it's to be honest about who you are and who the friends around you are.

Respect

One of my friends gave me a meaningful book as a wedding gift, *Love and Respect*.[24] I find the content in this book helpful in building all kinds of relationships. Love and respect begins at home; we then practice this everywhere we go. Respect boundaries and what matters to others, especially when you are in their home or space, although you may have your own set of ways.

Parenting expert Pam Leo points out: "We don't say, 'What do you say?' or 'What's the magic word?' to our friends, but children hear it all the time. If we expect children to always say please and thank you, we must always say please and thank you to them and to each other."[25] Children who see respectful behavior will imitate that respect.

That includes the measure of respect we demonstrate to those who hold leadership positions in our own lives. How do children hear you describe your boss, your pastor, their teachers? How do they see you behave in relation to these people? What does a child learn if their parents are rude to teachers? Some parents storm into school offices demanding, "Why didn't my child make an A?" If we choose to disrespect authority and disregard the rules set in place, our children will also do the same. Children are imitators, they don't have a mind of their own until their brains are fully formed. As surprising as it may sound, scientifically, our brain is not completely formed till we are 25 years old. So, this explains why we do what we do when we are younger, and this also explains why it's so important for us to be mentors and role models for the younger generation.

Love and Kindness

Whatever we practice on a daily basis tends to stick around with us and it eventually becomes part of our character. So being kind can come naturally once it's a habit just as being mean is a habit for some other people. Some kids practice being mean, sarcastic or rude to one another because it's something their classmates do in school. Do you know people who are disliked or who hardly have friends? If you study them closely, you will find that some of them have tendencies to poke fun and use words to joke in ways that often hurt those around them. The habits of people who are liked or disliked can be read through their interactions.

Habits are easily adaptable, so we must be intentional with our words and actions around people. Relationships are built through stages; we learn people as the years pass and we begin to understand what they are comfortable with and what bothers them. Once we understand a person, we can change our tone or the way we interact to build stronger bonds. For example, if someone told us that the words we used made them feel insecure or uncomfortable, we should refrain from using the words that made them feel that way. Joking about skin color or body weight may not be funny to those who view them as sensitive topics. We have to keep in mind that some people are more sensitive than others.

Showing kindness can be inconvenient. When we were on family road trips, my dad always stopped to assist accident victims or those whose vehicles had broken down. I remember waiting in the car for hours with my siblings and mom. It was frustrating to wait for hours in the car while my dad helped someone change a flat tire or wait until better equipped help arrived. As I've grown older, I have become more patient and empathetic in situations that require me to wait while someone is being helped. It has become almost like a habit to help someone in need.

Showing kindness can also take effort, especially for those who are not good at expressing themselves with words and actions. Many scholars are academically intelligent but not necessarily emotionally intelligent. Still, emotional intelligence reflects a set of habits that can be learned.

Kindness in Action

I appreciated my dad's habit of kindness the most when my car broke down in the middle of nowhere. I had been driving for miles and all I could see were open fields. I couldn't even tell what kind of crops were planted in them. I couldn't find any signs or landmarks.

I was stranded.

I tried calling my husband, but since he was at work, he didn't pick up the phone. I remember feeling lost and scared. When my husband called me back and asked me where I was, all I could say was, "I don't know."

While I was waiting, I prayed, "Jesus, please help me." A car pulled up next to me within seconds, and the two young boys inside asked if I needed help. I cautiously rolled down my window just a bit and told them that my help was on the way. They told me that they were on their way to church to deliver pizzas for the youth group but that they would come back to wait with me.

They came back after twenty minutes and waited in their car. My husband arrived an hour later – I can't imagine how he found me, but he did. The boys got out of their car and introduced themselves to my husband. Their names were Jesus and Joseph, if you can believe it. I still laugh when I tell people about it.

The experience reminded me of how I saw my dad behave when I was a child. These young boys were raised with kindness and a heart to help. They didn't have to wait with me, but they did. They'd apparently been trained in the habit of being kind.

We need kind people around us. It takes a little effort to practice kindness, but it goes a long way. Somehow, kindness is reciprocated, we reap what we sow. I am glad these boys were raised to help and show kindness.

Forgiving

We cannot forgive on our own without God's help. The habit of forgiving is important to sustain relationships: friendships, marriages, families, peers and colleagues.

My dad was a seasonal potter who was able to mold beautiful sculptures with his bare hands; it was one of his favorite pastimes. I wish I had pictures of his pottery work. I am, quite literally, a potter's child. My earthly, heavenly and spiritual father are potters, just different kinds of potters. I couldn't have picked a better title for this book.

Dad took my siblings and me to a pottery place, handed us clay, and showed us how he sculpted. While we made pots and bowls and played with clay just like kids would, he spent hours working on his almost life-size statue. Once completed, he would use a can of paint to spray all over it. We had a beautiful gold planter of a native man holding a pot. I remember that as a kid, I thought the sculpture looked like Tarzan—so masculine, with muscles and veins standing out as in Michelangelo's work. Those who have seen my Dad's sculptures will attest to the skill he had. The man had a gift.

Bishop T.D. Jakes (Potter's House Church) is my spiritual father, he is a potter who molds me through his books and teachings. *Let It Go* and his other books are my go-to's whenever I need God's help to forgive someone who has done me wrong.

God the giver of all gifts, on the other hand, is an even more amazing potter: a miracle-working potter. He is constantly working on molding and shaping us to live a purposeful life. God is the only potter who can help us attain the habit of forgiveness when we ask in prayer. Only He can turn sorrow to joy in a heartbeat.

When my sister contacted me about having discovered my dad after thirty years, I wasn't as excited as she was. But why? I longed to meet Dad again. I had so many questions to ask him. I had even practiced them in my head when I was little. I had watched my parents argue and physically fight and eventually one day my dad left and never returned home. But I'd never been able to ask why he never came back for us, his children.

After my sister told me she had found Dad, every memory I had of him was playing in my head for days. It was more like revisiting old wounds with deep scars that I never knew existed. Thirty years didn't seem long at all. Dad had many "valid" excuses, but none of his explanations mattered to me because he couldn't fix what was already shattered. A shattered pot that is put back together is not going to be the same, unless God intervenes and heals our heart.

Imagine struggling through childhood hungry, having no pretty clothes to wear, wearing donated school uniforms that were never the right size, standing in lines after school with the adults to pay the bills, carrying heavy bags of groceries with tender little hands, walking for miles because we didn't have a car after Dad left, having to work at a young age to help mom, missing out on Father's Day celebrations. These all came back in a flash of memories. My Mom, older sister, and I all had to work together to fill the role Dad walked away from. We struggled financially for years until Mom was able to give us a higher quality of living.

When we were young adults, my sister and I were both trapped in abusive relationships, fearing to walk away because we were afraid the abusers would hurt our families. I believed that we were treated that way because we didn't have a dad to protect us. It may not be true, but during the depths of all my fear and despair, it felt better to just blame it on someone and I blamed Dad. "If only Dad was around . . ." It also didn't help that, as the younger daughter, I had been "Daddy's girl," pampered by him. I remember Dad giving me all the change from his pockets, and holding me the entire night when I hurt my feet. What happened to all the love he had for us? I had many unanswered questions racing in my head. Unlike my friends and cousins who had their dads to walk them down the aisle on their wedding day, my mom walked me down the aisle. Dad was absent for too long. I was a married woman who had not known her father for decades.

The sorrow and pain hit all at once like a ton of bricks when Dad was suddenly back in the picture. Words cannot express how I actually felt. It was a hurricane of mixed emotions: hurt, anger, excitement, resentment, joy, anxiousness—all at once. One minute I was happy that I could reconnect with Dad and do things together that we had missed; another minute, anger and sadness overtook me.

Dad

Dad, I know your name, I carry yours

I wish you found me when I was lost

The years flew by, I crossed the shores

Life as usual is running its course

What do I say to you after thirty years

Should I speak love or about my fears

The wall I built has many spheres

Speeding heart beats, changing gears

If I could arrange words to communicate

They would help me to recuperate

A broken heart I could resuscitate

But the years lost, you cannot redecorate

Dad, I have loved you, I always will

Our Father in heaven has been my shield

When in doubt, he guides me to be still

I will talk when I am ready, that is the deal

Stephanie Mathews

When I was feeling excited to have dad back, I began choosing a birthday card for his upcoming birthday that year. "I can finally buy Dad a card for his birthday," I thought. I remember looking through the cards and not being able to find one that best fit him. "Dad, thank you for everything you do for us." Nope! "Daddy, you are our strength and support." Nope! "Happy Birthday to the best dad in the world." Nope! I was in tears as I read through the meaningful cards for dads who were present in their children's lives. I found a funny "old fart" card that couldn't make me laugh or smile, but that was the card I ended up buying for him. I left the store quickly while wiping away the tears that kept rolling down my cheeks.

I still have that card because when my emotions took over, I never followed through to mail it to him. I prayed and cried to my heavenly Father, the only potter who can mold my heart to make it whole again. I told God how difficult it was to forgive. Maybe I haven't forgiven my dad yet, and that's why I was still hurting. It had never bothered me the last thirty years. Why am I so upset now, I asked God. I needed to heal from wounds that were not completely healed. God helped me, though, as only He could.

By the time I traveled thirty-four hours to visit my dad and his new family, I was excited and had peace in my heart. I was able to embrace my brother, sister, and stepmom—my bonus family. Dad looked old and unrecognizable. He had gray hair, a shiny bald head, and a belly, but the same old cheeky smile. He didn't recognize me initially. When he knew who I was, we hugged each other tightly for a while and cried both happy and sad tears.

At that moment I knew that I had forgiven him, because I experienced nothing but joy to meet him and my new family. "I am sorry," Dad began, but before he could go on and on I was able to remind him about the things he taught me: dancing, driving, pottery, woodworking, painting. "Papa, remember this, remember that?" I asked. We had so much to catch up, I kept diverting his attention to all the good that he added in my life, the many good habits that I practice even today.

Forgiveness is not an easy habit to acquire. It takes faith and letting go. Our children are going to encounter moments where the hurt is unbearable and where forgiving seems impossible. Instead of revenge or getting back at others who hurt them, teach them to let it go, and teach them to forgive. If you need to learn this first, you ought to. Prayers helped me. Reading books helped me. Habits can be learned, practiced, and applied. Forgiveness is important in every single relationship. We will have disagreements and misunderstandings all the time with our parents, siblings, peers, friends, and people around us. But being able to forgive them will give us the peace we deserve. Things won't immediately fix themselves, because only time will heal, but first, we must forgive!

A lady whose son was involved in a shooting was sitting at opposite sides of the courtroom from the mother of her son's assailant. The dead boy's mother said she wished people knew that the other mother was hurting the same way. One lost her son and the other lost her son to his bad choices. Bad habits and bad choices will bring heartbreaks if we don't pay close attention to them. Forgiving in this context would probably be one of the hardest things to do if you were a parent who was grieving. Again, the habit of forgiving can be done with God's help. For many people, it takes years of healing and letting go.

Patience

I know someone who likes to be ready two hours before it's time to leave for any event. She stresses everyone out by reminding them over and over that she doesn't want to be late.

Being on time is a good habit. Being impatient is also a habit, and one that's not very helpful. Patience is a virtue worth pursuing, a habit we have to intentionally learn in this express era where everything is ready at the push of a button. We live in an instant world where conversations are timed and new machines are always faster than the ones we've had. I can wash and dry my clothes in one hour if I find that the outfit I want to wear is soiled. Everything in our world encourages impatience.

Still, it's important to slow down and breathe awhile. The habit of being patient is as important as the habit of being on time.

The Habits of a Friend

Part of what makes a friend are the habits that shape him or her as individuals. Self-care and self-evaluation are two important habits that mold us into the kinds of people who will be good friends.

Self-Care: Boundaries

We often think of self-care as the ways we give ourselves treats, rewards, and work breaks. Self-care also includes the ways we prepare ourselves for the tasks ahead and the ways we protect ourselves from needless problems.

My self defense instructor was a petite woman, and at the beginning of our first karate class, she fought a big guy. She took him down, and I was impressed. But when the lesson started, she gave us a different recommendation. Punch quickly, then run, she said. Because if you're not in the same place as your opponent, you won't get hurt.

This is important in situations that are hurting you physically and mentally. It's important for our sanity.

The Good Book says to forgive seventy-seven times. But what should we do when the same person hurts us over and over again? It's time to set boundaries. When kindness is taken for weakness, we can be hurt over and over. Never try to make sense to a fool. Just take your one (metaphorical) punch, then run.

Self-Evaluation

Have you heard country singer Blake Shelton's song "Who Are You When I'm Not Looking?" It describes a woman who is beautifully put together, but might be hiding things. The singer wonders if she rages in her anger, binge eats when she's sad, runs to her momma in frustration. He wants to know, who is she really?

Who is anyone really? Habits tell the story of who you really are. Good or bad, they make up your personality just like cells make up the human body. It's important to stay true to yourself and others even when no one is around. Integrity, honesty, and ethics are sought after in workplaces, so who you are matters even to your ability to make a living. If we put on a façade that we are honest when we are not, we won't be able to keep up with that for long.

Personality Tests to Try

The Enneagram Personality Test: Very popular right now, the Enneagram locates you among nine core personality types, indicating other types that potentially influence your behavior.

Myers-Briggs Type Indicator: Identifies you as one of sixteen personality types by categorizing you along four personality spectrums as either introvert-extravert, intuitive-sensing, feeling-thinking, judging-perceiving.

DISC Test: Assesses personality across the categories of Dominance, Influence, Compliance and Steadiness. This one is popular among many employers.

The Love Language Test: This test helps you recognize which of five ways to show love are your preferred ways to receive and give affection

I interviewed a candidate once who appeared pleasant and ready to learn, so I hired her. After a couple of months, she was no longer pleasant or teachable. She didn't want to take any instructions and began disrespecting the customers and her boss. Since I was flexible with her work hours, she began claiming more hours for jobs than her work required. When I first hired her, I had plans to make her a partner, but she ruined her opportunities by behaving the way she did. Bad habits can be seriously detrimental if they are not dropped. Some people have adopted the habit of being rude without realizing that it's a habit that will ruin many relationships, both personally and at work.

Personality tests can be a helpful way to self evaluate so that we can improve our habits. But of course we have to be truthful when we answer the questions built to analyze our personality. If you have not tried personality tests, you should. Many colleges recommend that students complete a personality test to self-evaluate and understand the level of commitment they are willing to put in.

Habits that Undermine Friendships

Having talked about many ways to nurture and grow friendships, I want to remind you of a few habits that undermine friendships.

Complaining

Have you heard of people complaining and whining about something or the other? Oh, it's so hot, oh, it's so cold. Oh this, oh that. Complaining is not only a bad habit but one that can ruin relationships. You can never please a chronic complainer. I am pretty sure you can think of someone right now. A chronic complainer is a person who will always find something to be unhappy about. They don't see the big picture of every situation; instead they harp on the small stuff.

Gossiping

There's a difference between sharing our pain with someone and gossiping. If someone hurt you and you want to talk about it, you should; however, avoid adding tension to the existing situation. Sometimes it helps a lot when you open up and talk to the right people. On the other hand, gossiping about people everyday and sharing random stories to many different people can become a habit that causes conflicts.

Have you heard of the Chinese Whisper game? You say "Police Officer" to your neighbor in Dallas, and by the time the whisper reaches New York, the word that's heard will be "Pehshersher." Gossip is that way, too. It gets misheard, twisted, and sometimes seasoned with exaggeration until it sounds absurd. It's best to avoid sharing rumors or whatever gossip you've heard.

Imitating

My neighbor walked up to my car one day as I was pulling up my driveway and told me that she noticed how beautiful the flowers in my flower beds were. She went on saying that she was planting the exact same colors of the same variety: yellow, orange, and red Plumed Castle celosia flowers. She then added, "Well, you know that imitation is a form of flattery." I thanked her and told her that the idea was not even mine. A friend who is an avid gardener suggested that I plant yellow Plumed Castle celosia so it would pop and look pretty next to my red brick walls, and I added the orange and red flowers to create a design.

My neighbor's approach was a positive form of imitation. We can all relate to her because most of us browse around for ideas before we decorate our homes or shop for clothes. I usually tweak the ideas I gather to personalize them, because I generally prefer adding my own touch to what I do. Still, there's nothing wrong with imitation until it becomes a negative trait. We are designed to be authentic, not a photocopy of anyone else. You be you, friend. God created only one of you for a reason. Even twins have different identities—something I can see even in my toddler babies. You don't need to copy what someone else has planned to do or keep up with the Joneses, because God's plans and the blueprint of your life is always going to be better than what you have for yourself.

"I am not creative; I have no ideas of my own." I have heard that way too many times before. When I owned a wood workshop store where patrons built wooden decorative pieces and painted them, many people claimed that they were not creative and didn't have any ideas. But guess what? These same people often walked out holding the most beautiful and creative pieces when they tried something on their own. People always doubt their creative abilities, not realizing that creativity is about being different, it's "one-of-a-kind" and that's what makes it special and valuable. Ten people can make the same farmhouse tray, yet leave with ten unique pieces with different colors and techniques. Be bold to be different.

The habit of imitating can be a put-off in relationships. It can make people uncomfortable and annoyed if you go overboard. Psychologists say that people who imitate others frequently have low self-esteem, a sense of worthlessness, and are envious. It's similar to identity theft because you are stealing someone else's uniqueness and fitting it into your lifestyle.

We often learn and do things similar to what our friends, relatives, or people around us do. Many people have similar interests, and it's common to like certain colors, clothes, brands, or hobbies. It's okay to use others as role models, but imitating almost every single thing someone else did, is doing, or plans to do becomes a negative characteristic or bad habit. So, if you have a bad habit of imitating a specific person all the time, you should stop, drop it, and focus on what's unique about you. The horse and zebra are uniquely created and each has a charm of its own. If you are a horse, accept galloping and be the horse you are meant to be. If you are a zebra, embrace your unique stripes, you are enough! Nobody compares a horse to a zebra; they are magnificent creatures on their own.

Choose Your Friends Wisely

We meet many different people throughout our lives, both good and bad. It's normal to have many friends when we are a young adult, because at that time being liked and popular is all we care about. As we grow older and know better, we choose friends wisely. We understand the importance of having quality friends who help us grow, share good and bad moments with us, and make good deposits in our trust bank.

If we stereotype people and shun people, our children will do the same. Have friends from all walks of life, race, religion and gender. Teach children to respect culture and differences. As a college student, I was burdened by realizing that one of my Muslim friends on campus was suicidal because nobody wanted to be his friend. He had been such a bubbly boy, but shut down and became very sad. He told me that people made rude and hurtful comments to him. His parents came to take him back to his home country. I was also appalled when a couple had two separate parties in their home, one for the "upper class" and one for the "low class." Even the food they ordered was different.

It's important to start this habit early of choosing friends who add value to your life and live by principles similar to those you follow. Principles are not necessarily based on race and religion. If you have a Muslim friend or a friend from a different social class who treats you with love and respect and has the qualities of a good person, he or she can be a lifelong friend.

Habits to Practice

Relationships are the most important part of our lives. If we cannot get along with family members, peers, neighbors and people we meet, we have to evaluate ourselves first. Listening, communicating, respecting, adapting, accepting changes and differences are some of the factors that contribute towards building good and lasting relationships. The classic How to Win Friends and Influence People by Dale Carnegie is a great book to read. We have to continuously work on improving our relationships and build a circle of people who have good morals and principles to mirror as we raise children. If you choose to hang around "troublemakers," you will eventually either learn their ways or your children will. One bad apple is enough to ruin the whole basket, as the saying goes.

A good way to practice this is to write your own eulogy or imagine your funeral. What would your family and friends say about you when you die? It sounds weird, but think about it this way: what value do you add by being in someone's life or not being in someone's life? Are people happier when you leave the room? If you miss an event, will people miss you or be glad that you didn't show up? If you leave nothing but bitterness in the hearts and minds of people who know you, it's time to be a Potter's Child. Practice good relationship habits; it's never too late.

Habits to Teach Children

Teach your children the importance of relationships from a young age because it will be difficult to learn certain habits when they are grown-ups. It's hard to teach an old dog new tricks. Your children will be surrounded by people in school, work and their new families. Their life with you should equip them to go out there and engage in meaningful relationships. You don't need to have a hundred friends to teach your child the habit of building relationships. You can start teaching them to respect their siblings and your spouse to begin with. Everything starts at home first: sharing, taking turns, communicating, forgiving, patience, kindness, boundaries, respect, and most important of all, love. A child who doesn't practice good relationship habits within a family is most likely to do the same wherever they go. We have to take this burden upon ourselves to help them in this area before they are depressed and confused at finding themselves disliked or avoided. Some parents are in denial and defensive, which won't help the situation because a child who is not corrected for disrespecting or being unkind will continue these habits which eventually will cause more damage to their lives.

A letter written by a death row inmate blamed his mother and her poor parenting for his plight.

Whether this is true or not, this letter is an eye opener.

"A death row inmate awaiting execution, asked as a last wish a pencil and paper. After writing for several minutes, the convict called the prison guard and asked that this letter be handed over to his biological mother.

The letter said …

Mother, if there were more justice in this world, we would be both executed and not just me. You're as guilty as I am for the life I led.

Remind yourself when I stole and bring home the bicycle of a boy like me? You helped me to hide the bicycle for my father did not see it.

Do you remember the time I stole money from the neighbor's wallet? You went with me to the mall to spend it.

Do you remember when I argued with my father and he's gone? He just wanted to correct me because I stole the final result of the competition and for that I had been expelled.

Mom, I was just a child, shortly after I became a troubled teenager and now I'm a pretty malformed man.

Mom, I was just a child in need of correction, and not an approval. But I forgive you!

I just want this letter to reach the greatest number of parents in the world, so they can know what makes all people, good or bad … is education. Thank you mother for giving me life and also helping me to lose it.

Your child offender."

Chapter 8

Time Management

When the clay is taken and carefully shaped, when the
care is awoken to beautifully make

A fine feeling of the patience cultivating a better light
that comes to undertake,

Every bit of what you endeavor, every effort, every tear,
every second sojourning

To the next, carrying in its wings a thousand splendid
dreams, daringly soaring

To horizons that expand before your eye, and you know
that the clock ticks away,

And you know that these times, so quick to leave, are
not here to stay...

And too many things to deal will keep you reaching for
less,

And too little to do will keep you in a filthy greed to toy
your heart to a mess...

So don't give in and don't give up... you have more to
give, more to do, more to dream,

And when you arrange the to-do list to the rhythm of a
reasoning to prioritize, you beam

With beauty! You'll be at ease, you'll know the catch,
you'll reach the goal,

Gear on, the great gamble of time is not for you to lose,
but to pitch it all for an eternal call...

Susan Ann Samuel

If you lose money, chances are you will be able to earn some back, but if you lose time, you will never recover it. As the poet wrote, "Time and tide wait for no man." You can never be fourteen or thirty-six again even if you had all the money in the world. That means it's essential to use our time well today, so our entire life will be filled with joy and purpose.

Time Management 24/7: The Elements of Your Organized life

Maybe when you think about time management you think about checklists that help you keep track of work or the kids' projects or home maintenance chores. But time management is about what we do with all the parts of our days. So when you think about managing your time, consider how you fit in all the basics of a satisfying, well-managed life.

We're surrounded with distractions of all kinds, amidst which we must learn to manage our time efficiently and productively to fulfill our goals. Strategies such as activating the do-not-disturb or silent mode on our digital devices while working on important tasks prevents distraction and contributes to productivity. Creating a daily schedule and blocking time for the day's activities, organized into chunks and spread out throughout the day, provides an efficient approach to tackling work.

- Physician-Scientist
  Dr. Sanya Thomas

Possession Care: Clean Up, Maintain

Part of your organized day is putting things away at the end of the day. To do this, it helps to practice getting things done, as we discussed in another chapter. It's much easier to put something away when you've reached some kind of stopping point.

Part of your organized life might also be deciding how much is too much to care for. For some parents, one way of reducing the cleaning and care burden might be deciding that all of the children's clothing should be fabrics that don't need ironing. Some families might choose to maintain a toy rotation for younger children, storing some toys for a few weeks so there are fewer toys and books to be put away daily. You can make the same kind of choices about how many clothes you keep in your own closet.

Managing Space to Manage Your Time

Organizing and tidying up is one of my favorite activities because it is so rewarding. The reward is being able to find what we are looking for when we need it most. Have you experienced that? If you know where to look for your documents, keys, even tea bags (Yes! tea bags!), you save yourself lots of difficulties.

You're probably laughing at the idea that it's important to know where your tea bags are kept. I had to mention this because my husband called me when I was visiting family out of state to ask me where we kept the tea bags. I could tell him where to look for them because they have their place, and now he knows.

My working experiences around the world gave me insights into different ways of keeping business documents organized. Although I have worked in offices big and small in Malaysia, Singapore, South Korea, London, and America, organizing is no different; the system is the same. Work in the hospitality and retail industries focused on presentation, whereas legal and advertising offices that provided client services focused on efficiency. There were slight differences in the strategies for staying organized, but the golden rule remains: everything has its place. Remember that mantra when it comes to creating your system. Trash goes where it belongs, documents should be filed, stationary should be replenished as it is used, all the extras have their own designated places, including the random drawer for the mumbo jumbo stuff

> *Anytime there is something you do repeatedly, such as filing papers, there is value in creating a SYSTEM (Saving You Space Time Energy Money) - Barbara Hemphill*

that lacks an assigned home.

I worked in an office that had five big boxes of closed files for all their customers. I remember how my colleagues and I dreaded looking through those big boxes, so we could find that one file we needed. It took effort and time that we could have spent on something else. When I completed organizing and labeling the files in filing cabinets, we were able to key in the name of the client and pull out the file from the cabinet within minutes. It made a complicated situation disappear just like that.

However, I later learned that the office did not maintain the system, so the boxes are back. Why is that? Because it takes initial effort to stay organized and it is a lot easier placing it in a random box. Good habits are important because if you don't make a point of practicing a good habit, the bad habit comes right back to get in your way.

In the same way, it's hard to find what you need in a chaotic home. You end up spending time looking for essentials that you'd rather invest in enjoying the people you love. Keeping things in order helps you make good use of your time.

Body Care: Eat, Drink, Exercise, Sleep

A purposeful and meaningful life cannot be achieved when health-related problems are caused by neglect and bad habits. Eating well, drinking water, exercising, and sleeping are all essential habits to practice because health is wealth.

What we feed our bodies is a priority, although many people only realize and make necessary changes when it is too late.

It's okay to enjoy that cake, but not every single day. I don't like to use the word "diet" because the more I say it, the more deprived I feel, so I just eat everything in moderation. That solves all my cravings and it helps me be in control. That way I don't have to shy away from my favorite dessert or scrumptious meal. It is tempting to finish an entire bowl of ice cream. If eating right is a challenge for you, I can relate. But remember, our minds are powerful and you can learn to talk yourself out of it. My husband once said that dieting is all in the mind, it's all about self-control, and that's so true. We are powerful creatures and our minds have the power to help us achieve what we want, including eating a well-balanced nutritious meal.

Mom cooked when she was a homemaker, and she cooked when she worked; she managed her time to fit in cooking. It was just a habit. We had well-balanced, healthy, home-cooked food for almost every meal.

When my sister and I were teenagers, Mom wanted us to learn this important life skill. So she wrote recipes on a piece of paper and left detailed cooking instructions for us to follow before she left for work every day. When I moved away to live on my own for college, these skills came in handy. Still, I didn't master cooking immediately. I remember adding too much ginger to my chicken curry once, and another time I cooked it so spicy that my friends' eyes teared up and their ears were smoking! It was hideous.

My aunty and my grandmother cooked with ease, like Mom. My grandma made her herbal soup, rasem, without a recipe, and I learned to make it myself by working alongside her, pounding the black pepper and coriander seeds in a mortar before they were added to the pot. On a cold winter's day, rasem is the best thing to have. It keeps the body warm with all its rich ingredients, soothing aroma, and tomato flavor filled with Indian spices. When my husband has a cold, rasem is what he wants, because the ingredients include turmeric, an anti-inflammatory agent. I cooked rasem for friends who visited from Malaysia for Christmas, years ago. The winter was biting cold that year but we stayed warm and cozy with our hot bowl of rasem.

For a long time, I thought it was easier for the older people to cook. Then, I lived with a friend in London for a short while. When she returned home after work, we had our tea time together. She would make me a cup of a robust, rich PG Tips tea, a very popular British tea brand. Our tea time moments were special, but what I'll never forget was her impressive skill in cooking four dishes for dinner while sipping her tea. She looked like a professional chef at work. She chopped the veggies and onions, placed a pot on each of her stove's four burners, added water and spinach to one, oil to another, dal (split lentils) to a third, and potatoes to the fourth, and she kept cooking while engaging in conversation with me. My eyes were fixed on the pots and pans because I was afraid she was going to burn one of her dishes. She, on the other hand, was as cool as a cucumber, swaying around her kitchen as if getting four dishes cooked while chatting was easy peasy. I watched her serve her husband his dinner with love and grace—it was simply beautiful, and a habit I wanted to learn. She was in her late 20s and had lived most of her teenage life without a mother because her mom passed away during the Sri Lankan war. Her dad did all the cooking, and she learned the habit of cooking from him.

Cooking isn't easy. It's hard work, and just as with everything else worthwhile, practice makes perfect. Still, cooking is a good habit to have, and it looks simple and easy when it's a habit; that's my point. All these people who mastered this art are people who did it repetitively. The more we cook, the more we learn, and there's joy in exchanging recipes and trying out recipes from other ethnic groups.

Why cook? Well, because you are in control of the ingredients and can make healthy choices. We are in control of the amount of oil we use, the type of meat, spices, etc. Serving a balanced diet is important, one containing includes carbs, vegetables and fruits, protein, fat, fiber, grains, and water. My mom cooked pureed food for all her toddler grandchildren when she cared for them. I learned that from her, too. We had both home cooked food and store-bought food for the babies.

Health was my mother's priority. She made us drink lots of water, eat fruits and vegetables, and maintaining a well-balanced diet was important. She would bring us a couple of almonds as snacks to munch on when we were at our table studying, and I remember her asking, "Did you drink water today?"

Even though I am much older now, Mom's words and habits linger within me. I value them because they allow me to live a healthy life. Some days I don't drink enough water and begin to feel dehydrated and fatigued, and although my mom lives thousands of miles away, I can almost hear her ask, "Did you drink water today?"

Many people are not privileged to have someone in their life who teaches them to eat right or practice good, healthy eating habits, but books and resources online can be great guides. I learned many new recipes through a book when I first began feeding my twins solid food. You will be thankful that you learned the habit of eating right. And it won't just make you look good, it will also make you feel good.

It's almost a seasonal dilemma for me to actively practice the habit of exercising. I admire my husband's ability to stay true to himself in this area ever since I have been married to him. "I must get back to the habit of exercising," I tell myself all the time and yet fail to meet this goal sometimes. Babies and endless responsibilities get in the way, cloud the idea of exercising, but again exercise is a habit. Exercise is proven to increase energy, decrease anxiety and depression, and improve blood circulation. We know that exercise can keep us fit and has countless benefits. Whatever you do, stay active!

I have to admit that the only reason I am fit today is because I am always on the move running after my twin toddlers. I can't tell you if it replaces cardiovascular exercise. Nevertheless, they keep me chasing them to the east and west.

When our body is stationary, we invite many unnecessary illnesses. Slow blood circulation, body aches and pain are symptoms that are contributed to being a couch potato, and being a couch potato is just a habit. Although many people know the consequences of being inactive, their habits anchor them to poor health. As the saying goes, "You can take the horse to the water, but you can't make it drink." Nobody can force someone to change or to adapt a good habit. This cycle can be broken with willpower and extra effort.

> *Although many people know the consequences of being inactive, their habits anchor them to poor health.*

Getting enough sleep isn't easy for any of us; and getting active young children to bed can be a special challenge, pediatrician Dr. Elizabeth R. Thomas notes. Here are some simple steps she suggests to help your little ones have a healthy sleep routine:

1. Avoid screen time 1-2 hours before bedtime.

2. Dim or turn off all lights in the room.

3. Limit fluids for two hours before bedtime.

4. Put your child to bed at the same time every night and have them wake up at the same time each morning.

5. If your child gets up, simply put the child back in bed and stand by the door of the room to monitor for a few minutes. Reassure your child that you are close by.

How much should your child sleep? According to the Journal of Clinical Sleep Medicine,[26] Dr. Thomas notes, these are the recommended hours:

1. 4-12 months of age: 12-16 hours of sleep per 24-hour period (including naps)

2. 1-2 years of age: 11-14 hours per 24-hour period (including naps)

3. 3-5 years of age: 10-13 hours per 24-hour period (including naps)

4. 6-12 years of age: 9-12 hours per 24-hour period

5. 13-18 years of age: 8-12 hours per 24-hour period

The next time you're putting your kids to sleep, take a deep breath and remember these simple steps. If you are concerned that your child may have a more serious problem, like sleep apnea, please contact your child's doctor.

Community Care: Volunteering

The habit of volunteering and doing simple acts of kindness go a long way. Its making time for our soul. Our time can be used to live a meaningful and purposeful life and our simple gestures can impact lives around us. Besides pouring in time and love towards our family, we can also invest time to make someone else's life a little better. Teach your children not to be consumed by themselves and just your family. It doesn't matter if you don't have enough money to donate, your precious time can be a blessing to someone in need.

Teaching our children to volunteer is a beautiful and rewarding habit. I have friends who travel to less fortunate countries every summer with their families to serve the poorer communities. Some take up big projects helping their church to build homes from the ground up in some small villages. These projects require both labor and skills. Certain skills that we learn in service to others will bless us in return over our lifetimes.

One of the skills I learned while volunteering is how to care for horses. My love for animals and children led me to become a volunteer at Equest Therapeutic Horsemanship in Dallas. Horse therapy helps children and injured veterans improve their motor skills and supports their socialization. Just riding a horse brings joy to some of these children who hardly communicate. Their coos and giggles are among the best gifts the horses give the children's parents.

Before we could start, we were trained for a few weeks to groom the horses, saddle the horses and walk the horses. These training sessions were necessary to help us understand and learn about these majestic creatures. Horses are sweet, they are playful, and they have their own personalities. During my volunteer sessions, ten horses were lined up to walk on a trail for forty-five minutes with special needs children riding. I always felt like I was walking big dogs, although caring for horses -- especially cleaning their hooves -- can be a little challenging. Every time I drove home after volunteering, I smelled of the barn, but my heart was so full it didn't matter.

Being a volunteer is humbling because we are serving without getting any monetary return. Children who volunteer become selfless and are willing to go the extra mile without expecting anything in return. Teaching children to help an elderly neighbor mow the lawn or to visit the sick produces meaningful habits that will eventually be passed on to their own children, making a difference in even more people's lives.

Relationship Care: Pay Attention to People Who Matter

Your children won't be children forever, so spend quality time with your family, eat dinner together, pray together, play board games, sing and dance, travel and go for picnics. Little things and big things done together build bonds and create lasting memories.

Likewise, spend quality time with friends and people you love. You can't build friendships and relationships if you are not willing to invest your time.

Joy Care: Hobbies and Pastimes

Do you have a hobby? What do you do with your extra time? Aren't we the luckiest people to have YouTube, which is a heaven for hobbies in this day and age. I've learned different guitar strumming patterns, new recipes, how to crochet, different languages and much more with the help of YouTube.

Whatever interests you, try it when you have a little time. Help children discover their hobbies by exposing them to different things. I love watching my children Sophia and Jude play on the piano or strum the guitar while singing their nursery rhymes. Although they go off tune all the time, I do hope that they find their own favorite hobbies someday and keep enjoying the sound of music.

Soul Care: Spending Time with God

Throughout my teenage years, young adulthood and even before having children, I was able to allocate some time every morning to read devotional books and pray. Praying doesn't always mean asking God for something; it also means connecting with God and thanking Him for all the blessings of life, including the trials. "Lord, I don't know why I am going through this frustrating period, are you trying to teach me something?" I talk to God and He talks to me, too. He talks through people and signs; He always responds. However, it requires us to be humble and pay attention.

Nowadays, I talk to God on the go when I am driving to the grocery store or waiting in line at the bank or while watching my children play. I am unable to dedicate a certain time everyday because my responsibilities keep shifting. Nonetheless, taking time to pray keeps me afloat when my day gets chaotic. Spend time to meditate, or do something else that keeps your mind sound. Be still and take time to calm yourself down from the hustle and bustle of your life and allow yourself to recharge. You won't be able to teach children this habit unless you know how to handle your sanity yourself. I know how to because every time my days get crazier than planned, I turn to God for help and He always comes through by showing me a way. Don't ask me how I get it done: ask God. I wouldn't be able to handle a day without prayer.

Habits to Practice

Consider your time as if it's money: something precious that can be lost forever. If you fail to allocate time to enjoy and play with your children or spouse, someday you will regret it. They will be consumed with their own agendas and friends, and they won't look to you for time or attention.

Your best investments are not necessarily related to money. They're related to time. Time builds relationships, time heals, time manages your tranquility. Managing time is mastering almost every aspect of your life. Time well spent will give you more returns than money can give you.

Living a balanced life requires the habit of time management.

Habits to Teach Children

Children will mirror you and your time management habits. Give them quality lessons by modeling good use of time to do all the things that make for a good life. Let them practice, as you do, a balanced life where they work, learn, love others, strengthen body and soul, and play.

Help children manage their time by creating a schedule chart and placing it on the wall, especially during exams and the school year. This will help them manage time to study and take leisure breaks.

Chapter 9

Read and Learn

No one will feed your thoughts with power, if not you,

And power is not an outburst uncontained: it is a slow taming of the mind through

Every ache of uncertainty... and when you touch your pen, when you feel the paper,

When each word wields a veracity empowering you to a deeper

Thought, then think, read and learn! Your wings will find their color and you'll fly,

There's a world out there, and there are children just wishing for a piece of paper. They cry.

This is your moment, your miracle. You've got everything you need to be unstoppable,

The fingerprints of the Potter in you are love, grace, wisdom... and all things are possible!

So child, take courage when you're on the Potter's wheel and the motion forms you gradually,

The world awaits the person you're becoming... so pursue for them, for yourself, for the world... intentionally,

Be mindful of your future, be merciful to your past, and make each moment that comes your way to stay,

Build precision, beckon it with reason, get back to the basics. Learn, read, write, speak, and don't look back... go all the way!

Susan Ann Samuel

My two-year-old repeats every Spanish word her nanny says, so I've learned a couple of words in Spanish just from hearing her chatter. I benefited from that small, seemingly random language lesson when I was at an event where my table's waitress didn't speak English. I cobbled together the words I knew and pointed to a white sugar packet. "Mas blanco" (more white), I said. She understood! I got my cup of sweetened coffee.

I never thought learning colors in Spanish with my child would come in handy, but it did. Continuous learning improves the quality of life we have; it adds value in many forms. You are never too old to form the habit of learning. In fact, to stay sharp and maintain a good memory, the brain must be constantly active. An active mind will keep us healthy. After all, "an idle mind is the devil's workshop" so, remember to keep your mind active and stay away from trouble. Trouble will find you if your mind is up to no good.

Learning Never Stops!

Teachers and mentors are all around us. Learning is a habit, and when you have the habit of learning, your mind will always look for opportunities to keep learning. We can learn

Self-development is a great investment;

it's an investment you make in yourself.

something new almost everyday, making the habit of learning as important to our health as food. A sound body alone is not fit to accomplish anything. A sound mind is the key to a long life.

Self-development is a great investment. It's an investment you can make in yourself. Learning should become a habit considering the advantages of knowing something new. Our brain is exactly like a muscle that will perform better when it remains active. Knowledge is powerful, and the best part about learning something is the fact that you cannot unlearn it. If you get a chance to learn something, do it. It will be worthwhile. Some of us are blessed to have mentors who take us under their wings to mold and shape us, while others are not so lucky. Whether or not you have a mentor who is present in your life, you can begin outsourcing the help you need to improve yourself.

We no longer have excuses when it comes to resources. We live in the technology era loaded with information, so it's our responsibility to continue learning and developing ourselves, even if we are not blessed to have a one-on-one mentor.

Years ago, I took a job in London. My bosses were keen to open a salon offering facials, hairstyling and other cosmetic services. As I began assisting them, I had to learn about the legal aspects of operating the business. To obtain a license to operate a cosmetology-based business, I was asked if I was willing to study cosmetology. Agreeing to study cosmetology in India was one of the best decisions I made; studying in India also made for the most challenging months of my life. I was close to throwing in the towel because I had to sacrifice all the comfort I was accustomed to in London.

Does it sound funny to say that I had culture shock when I first went to India? Although my maternal grandparents were from India, they migrated to Malaysia, and I was born in Malaysia. India was foreign to me, it was humid, and the noise of constant honking gave me headaches. I was used to working in London. I paused for a long time whenever someone asked, "Where are you from?" It took quite a long explanation to describe how I ended up in India studying cosmetology.

As challenging as I found that experience, the lessons I learned as a manager of that small business ultimately equipped me to open and operate my small business in Dallas. Although some of the steps were different, the fundamentals of operating a small business were the same. Every lesson learned in life will come in handy someday. Knowledge is like treasure hidden in every nook and corner, if only we embrace the habit of learning.

Where to Seek Learning

One of my favorite quotes is, "When the student is ready, the teacher will appear." Are you ready to learn? Where will you find your teachers?

People You Know

I learned many valuable skills from my parents, siblings and extended family. One of my uncles taught me the importance of learning every chance we get; he taught me the importance of music theory, how to use chopsticks, how to spell difficult words, the times table, and much more. Another uncle taught me how to ride a motorbike when I was a teenager. I remember how I

Lessons from my Grandmother

Grandma's home became my second home after my parents separated. My two siblings and I were cared for and raised by my grandma when my mom began working.

I have walked for miles with her carrying packages of food to feed the prisoners she visited. I remember walking to the hospital with her to meet random strangers whom she prayed for, ward by ward. I remember the aroma in her kitchen when she cooked for the entire family. I cherish her herbal soup recipe. I remember helping her rake leaves and tend to her plants.

My grandma was a little cranky at times but that was probably the only flaw she had. I love her dearly and miss her, for she taught me many valuable life lessons that I hold close to my heart.

loved the wind blowing on my hair as we rode around a big field. My aunties taught me how to care for myself when I was a teenager. One taught me basic personal hygiene; another taught me and my sister how to use makeup when we were young adults. My dad taught me how to drive in his Mini Cooper and he taught me how to ballroom dance. I remember how he held my hands and taught me how to waltz around the house. "Two steps to the right, and two steps to the left", he would say as we danced to the rhythm of the music. Mom and grandma taught me countless life lessons as homemakers, even while holding a job.

My brother taught me perseverance. I have watched him grow up to be a responsible father to a son by working hard and keeping his chin up, despite the many struggles life has thrown at him. My dad never embraced him because when my brother was born, he was considered bad luck, according to the astrology priest my dad talked to. I remember the abuse that my brother had to endure when dad was not good to him; he was not even allowed to cry like a little boy. Sometimes when I watch my husband show affection to my toddler son and hold his hands to play with him or even fondly call him "son," It takes me back to the life my brother had as a toddler, and it saddens me that he was never treated with love that way. A boy needs his dad! My mom tried filling in dad's shoes. She would treat him extra special growing up, and my sister and

I called him "the favorite child" with annoyance, but it didn't bother us as much because he was the baby of our family then and we loved him. Life in school didn't do him right either, he was a victim of bullying. My sister and I had our own share of struggles to deal with; we were never able to help him with his. It was tough growing up as a teenage boy without a dad present; his friends were his only guy companions. My brother was always searching for something. He had a restless spirit and big dreams, and he ventured into many different areas as an adult: deejaying, real estate, car salesmanship, owning businesses. He is a self-taught and self-made man. He failed many times, lost money, got cheated, hit bump after bump, but he stands tall and he teaches me the habit of endurance. I cannot be any prouder as an older sister.

As soon as you leave your family house, the world is your teacher. From teachers in school to your peers, they are all mentors if you care to pay attention. Some of my classmates knew more about certain subjects because of their parents or older siblings. If we rely solely on what we are taught, our knowledge and wisdom will be limited. However, when we practice the habit of learning, we automatically are ready to learn all the time. Every form of lesson will benefit us.

Sunday Sermons in church taught me many lessons, my church pastors (Trinity Church Dallas) share many life experiences, both theirs and of others. I keep my notes for years because everytime I look back, it's like discovering hidden treasure; I find something new to learn from it. With years of working experiences in different parts of the world and different work settings, I have learned immensely from my bosses. I had the honor of working for many different bosses who had different styles, but most of them inspired me to keep learning something new. One of my bosses gave me an opportunity to be part of Microsoft training in the 90's when Powerpoint, Word, and Excel were newly launched. Although the stock exchange firm I worked for was only going to send the management staff, when I knocked on his door and asked him if he would consider sending me, he smiled and agreed. "What are you going to do with the knowledge?" he asked, since I was just a receptionist then. I said that I could help out the other departments. Although he passed away in a freak car accident years later, I will never forget him because the opportunity he gave me to learn allowed me to participate in a t-shirt designing competition for the firm, which I won. It also helped me get promoted to the Training and Education Department where I was assisting by invigilating exams for remisiers and giving the opening and closing speech to introduce each speaker for the training.

Another boss noticed that although I was a hard worker, I lacked social skills. I often declined invitations to socialize with my peers. My lack of knowledge in winning friends caused tension at work because the supervisor had her favorites and I was not one of them. I was not interested in joining my colleagues for dinner because I had my own circle of friends, but that didn't help with building relationships at work. I didn't realize the importance of building relationships in every setting. My boss bought me Dale Carnegie's book, *How to Win Friends and Influence People,* and he told me that the book would change my life—and he was right! I also had another boss who believed in me and gave me a book by Zig Ziglar as a birthday gift, entitled *See You At the Top.* In it, he wrote, "See you at the Top, Champ!" I learned to dream big from him, and recently when I reconnected with him on social media I thanked him for encouraging me and inspiring me. One of the most important lessons I have learned about organizational skills and the habit of following a system was from my boss who was an attorney. Her penchant for showcasing spectacular organizational skills and maintaining a detail-oriented setting was a habit I admired. There are many more I could mention, but the point is to accept constructive feedback and be open to learning, because as you can see, each person we encounter influences us with their good habits.

Learn from the elderly, they have years of experience compared to you. You may be really good with technology or in preparing the greatest resume, but the perspective and wisdom gained by the elderly are achieved by undergoing many challenges and learning many lessons throughout their lives. If you pay close attention, the lessons they learned by experience will help pave your way in life. The older you grow, you will realize that the less you know. Nobody knows enough.

If you ask a 90-year-old person what they do on a daily basis, you will find out that besides eating right, sleeping right, and exercising, they also keep their mind sharp by learning something, actively using their brain muscles.

Books, Conferences, Podcasts: Learning from People You Haven't Met

Thank goodness for Google. We enjoy an ocean of resources. When I first dove into business endeavors, I started following many business owners on social media. The more people I followed, the more I learned. Just by following a couple of entrepreneurs, I was exposed to books, materials and conferences they recommended based on their experiences. If you don't know where to look or how to look for something, ask around. We have to be humble to learn a thing or two. Your friend or relative may know something. It's okay to ask even if you think it will sound silly. Whenever I find myself feeling embarrassed to ask a question about something I don't know, I remind myself the famous Chinese proverb which goes, "The man who asks a question is a fool for a minute, the man who does not ask is a fool for life."- Confucius

Inculcating the habit of reading in childhood reaps many benefits in adulthood, Physician-Scientist Dr. Sanya Thomas notes. "Parents who read to their babies raise children interested in books, helping them develop strong communication skills critical for academic and professional success. Reading aloud activates multiple neurosensory pathways and helps a child develop focus and critical thinking. It's also beneficial to teach children more than one language, because their rapidly developing brains develop the skill quickly, and eventually, children find that knowing multiple languages is extremely helpful later in life, Dr. Thomas notes. She also touts the value of cursive handwriting, which she describes as "a dying art that has incredible potential for development of gross and fine motor skills."

IQ and EQ: Inborn Abilities, Skills to Learn

You are born with your IQ. Your intelligence and intellectual potential are in your DNA, but don't be disheartened if you are not the smartest kid in your class. The smartest kid may not be skillful in certain areas where you have skills. I honestly don't know who has the higher IQ: my husband the doctor who knows how to care for cancer patients or my gardener who knows how to care for all the plants in our yard. What matters about IQ is using what you have to the best of your ability for good purpose.

Our children are born with certain abilities and certain limitations, and it is okay to acknowledge and guide them to focus on their abilities. Comparing our children with others can add unnecessary pressure to them to live up to others when they are not able. Here's a story to better understand this.

When I was twelve, I studied in a Christian school in a small town. There I met a few friends who were very clever. They were always the top students in class. I looked up to them and 12-year-old me always felt that they were "so cool."

When we moved to a different city, I kept in contact by writing letters, but after several years, we lost touch. Years went by and we were living in different countries, but fate allowed me to reconnect with one of those friends. I was working in Singapore as a hotel manager, and my daily routine included going through my list of VIPs checking in. I drafted welcome letters for each one, ensured that a fruit basket and wine were placed in each of their rooms, and checked the rooms to make sure every detail had been taken care of by the housekeeping department.

As I was typing one of the VIP names, I noticed it looked familiar. It was the exact same first name, middle name and last name of one of my classmates from years before. Could it be a coincidence? A soft prompting in my heart made me type out a different letter. I wrote, "Dear Ms... (I can't believe it's not you), we are honored to have you as our guest today. It is such a coincidence that you share the same name with my long lost childhood friend. Were you a student at the (Small Town School)? If you were, kindly leave me your contact information, I would love to catch up with you. If you just happen to share the same name my sweet friend had, please disregard this letter and please accept my apologies." I signed off and left to go home after my long day's shift.

The next morning I was welcomed with a pleasant surprise. "Oh Stephanie, it was such a delight to hear from you! I can't believe this, fate sure does amazing things, please call me!!! " She left her contact information and we did a lot of catching up. We were both approaching our thirties and we shared from where we had left off: teenage years, relationship dramas, friends, family etc. We laughed out loud, cried both happy and sad tears, shared some heartbreaking life experiences and had deep conversations that left me pondering as I sat in the train to head back to my apartment. I couldn't believe how "the cool kid" I knew had attempted suicide from her apartment balcony. She said that she had wanted to end the misery of always needing to achieve high academic goals to keep her parents happy.

I don't really know if some parents realize the stress they put their children through when they have overly high academic expectations. It's important for the child to know that they don't need to accomplish things to make their parents happy.

Intelligence is a gift, high or low. People with a high IQ can find themselves in emotional distress and so can people with a low IQ. We have to embrace our own capabilities and make the best of what we are born with. This journey in life is not a competition. We can all be winners. The stage is big enough for everyone to celebrate their successes.

> *Life is not a competition. The stage is big enough for everyone to celebrate their successes.*

Emotional intelligence, unlike IQ, is a set of skills that can be learned. Just like everything else, its many habits can be learned and practiced till they become part of our lives. Emotional intelligence is a sought-after skill-set by many organizations. When we hold a job or are part of an organization, we are called to perform no matter what we are going through. Unfortunately, many people are unable to control their emotions. Failure to practice the simple habit of emotional self-control can make or break relationships and be a deal breaker in workplaces.

Almost everybody has good and bad days. I remember breaking down once when my boss was unhappy about a mistake I made at work. I started sobbing, not because she had corrected me, but because at that moment, my entire adoption process had failed and I couldn't concentrate on my job. I was inconsolable. I explained to her and she empathized and told me to take the day off. It's not easy to compartmentalize emotions, at times. The important thing is to learn ways to make emotional intelligence become a habit. At a moment when I could not manage emotional self-control, my boss projected emotional intelligence when she allowed me to take a break.

Emotional intelligence is also important in other situations. If you know someone who constantly belittles you or upsets you and nothing you do could help change the situation, it's time to set boundaries. For many, it's easier being a people pleaser than setting boundaries. This habit became easier for me as I grew older. I used to be a people pleaser, hoping that I would be liked and included. I was willing to tolerate disrespect and people who constantly made me feel uncomfortable with their bad intentions. Then something clicked in my brain one day. It was like a switch overnight. I decided to set boundaries. Perhaps it takes time and many experiences to teach us some habits.

Another form of emotional intelligence I had to learn relates to perfectionism. I used to be a perfectionist, and it bothered me when I couldn't achieve the results I wanted. Nobody would be mad at me but myself. It's as if I had a compulsively obsessing twin. Although I am detail-oriented in some ways, my left brain and my right brain are always battling with each other. I had to learn that sometimes good enough is good enough, and then practice it until I made it an emotionally intelligent habit.

How to Make Learning a Habit

When our minds are ready to learn, we don't need to schedule time to learn something new every day. It will become a habit to look for something new to read or listen to. We can make an intention to nourish our minds by reading a magazine or an article online or watching a YouTube video until we do it without putting any thought into it. Even if we don't read something everyday, we will look for something new to learn constantly because it will be part of our nature to do so.

In that way, learning is just like watching TV. If TV watching is a habit, you will automatically grab your favorite snack and binge watch your favorite series day after day. There's nothing wrong with doing that, but if that habit gives your body aches and sluggish thinking, it will affect your health and mental state. Our bodies are designed to be active mentally and physically, so being inactive will cause unnecessary health issues… and it can also add gloominess to your mood. Happy people are not people who have perfect lives. They're people whose habits are the happy juices that fuel their lives.

I remember looking for books to read about happiness when my engagement with my ex-fiance ended. I do believe that God helped me to find that book when I prayed. I remember how a book helped me bounce right back. If you don't know something, learn about it. We are so blessed to have resources available to us through the internet now compared to when the library which was the only place we relied for various resources. I wouldn't recommend self medicating or self diagnosing by using Google, but self-help is available. Nobody knows you better than you, and there are times when none of the counselors out there will be able to pull you out of the rut you're in. However, if you are willing to look for a remedy in a book, you will find one that best fits you.

> *Happy people are not people who have perfect lives. They're people whose habits are the happy juices that fuel their lives.*

When my second attempt at in-vitro fertilization failed and I was beat up emotionally, I realized that my husband who loved me dearly couldn't understand my grief. The book Men are from Mars and Women are from Venus[27] reminded me that we women are emotional creatures and men are more often technical when it comes to managing emotions.

I remember desperately looking for a book to help me endure the IVF (In vitro fertilization) process the third time. By then, I was mentally prepared to adopt two puppies if I didn't get pregnant! But God showed up and answered my prayer to be a mom. Being pregnant with twins was the best surprise, but I was also petrified as to how I would handle two babies at once. I bought all the books available about raising twins: You Can Two; Twins 101; Healthy Sleep Habits, Happy Twins; Raising Twins and more. I have the best books on my shelf that taught me many valuable lessons. Of course, the books are just a guide. Every child is different and we cannot solely rely on books alone. The habit of learning is rewarding either way.

Helping Children Learn

Children learn as we teach them and as they watch us. Again, the best way to teach a child is by living out what they need to learn. This has to be ingrained in our minds.

Children pick up everything they observe. Unfortunately, when they are very young, they don't know any better. They imitate what they see and don't quite understand the fuss we make about their bad behavior. This is something most parents will encounter every now and then. Their children's behavior is altered once they attend school or a different setting. I started noticing my toddlers became more aggressive with each other after they spent time in daycare. It's the parents' consistent training and modeling of different behavior that will make the difference.

My nephew once learned a bad word from school and started using it freely at home. Although it is common for some families to use curse words at home, it wasn't something any of us dared to do because my mom wouldn't tolerate it. I heard my nephew say, "But the boy in school said it. It's not a big deal, mom." I heard my sister respond: "The boy in school doesn't live here. We don't talk like this at home, so quit saying it. We speak to each other with respect in this house."

Children need to be taught kindness. It's a habit many lack these days. Kindness includes acknowledging and greeting one another, being patient, sharing, taking turns, visiting the sick, helping a neighbor, cheering a friend on, lending a helping hand, motivating and offering comfort. Learning a new skill benefits the individual, but the habit of kindness benefits everyone your child encounters. When children have the habit of being kind, it's difficult for them to unlearn it unless they are influenced by bad company. However, when they are surrounded by bad company, remind them to be a Potter's Child. A Potter's Child will pick the good habit and drop the bad. Even bad company might have one good habit, and that's all we should focus on. "Bad company" could even be influenced for the good by watching your child. That's the goal, to practice and model good habits.

There is a reason why certain materials and movies are PG13 or are rated appropriate for children to read and watch. It is because children are like sponges. It is best to feed them the information that can be beneficial to them as they mature. Any negative form of material will remain in their system for a long time just like the bad cholesterol stuck underneath the layers of our skin which we call love handles. But love is blind; we overlook the bad habits that our children possess and sometimes take it lightly. Bad habits that are not dropped can cause damage to a person's personality just like the love handles that can turn into health issues. Surround children with age appropriate materials and people who enrich them.

Habits to Practice

Read every chance you get. Watch videos, documentaries, listen to podcasts, teach yourself cooking, gardening, music, knitting, art, writing, poetry, games... pick your interest and follow it! It's okay to binge watch movies, but tune into something educational sometimes: documentaries and channels where you gather knowledge about something you never knew. Your interest may lie in hunting or app building, you may like geography and horses, but learning about something all the time will enrich your life. Books have a unique way of adding value to our lives. If you prefer audio books or a different learning method, the internet is flooded with information. Use it. Stay well informed about technology, sports, and world news. Learn about good habits. Even if you are not well traveled, you can learn about any topic via the internet these days. This is also an excellent way to stay connected with people. We are able to connect with people based on mutual interest. Learning is a bridge to many avenues. Be willing to teach whenever you get the chance; you retain what you know even better when you teach it. So, impart your knowledge to help and inspire others.

Habits to Teach Children

Reading to and with your child will foster the love of learning in your children. When you make reading a habit, your children will follow after you. Having said that, it's important to find out how your child learns best. I am a visual learner. I know other people who prefer listening to podcasts. When we enjoy learning and give ourselves the chance to learn in ways we enjoy, it will be an exercise we will repeat. Teach children what you have learned, encourage them to learn something new every chance they get, show them where to look for learning resources, guide them and give them the exposure that will help them adapt the habit of learning. Learning to write is also an important habit to acquire as it will serve them throughout their lives through school and form of application processes. Technology skills will allow children to learn things more quickly, find new ways to learn, and locate instruction for skills they want to master. It is a privilege to teach our children and in return learn something from them. As long as we have the habit of learning, we will enjoy this journey as they grow.

Chapter 10

Dream Big

The clouds won't stay shady for long,

I know your eyes are already seeing the silver lining,

There's no special recipe to be strong,

It's just you knowing you need to keep going...

Dream Big!!!

Oh Potter's Child!! So lovingly held in grace, be confident in believing,

That the trees shall sway, the wind shall blow, the leaves will flutter on the brown twigs,

And you'll know that the only thing that kept you sturdy and keeps you strong is your faith in perceiving

The unseen, knowing the unknown and exploring the uncharted territories.

The World will try to dim your light, and odds may storm at your tender flame,

But know this, child... keep shining, even though you flicker for a moment... know the stories

Where grace has fanned the flame to free the World in Love's name!

And YOU are creating history! So dream big!

Susan Ann Samuel

As a child raised by a single mom and working to help pay the bills, I was constantly daydreaming because that was the only thing I could afford to do. I dreamed I was flying away on a plane. I dreamed I was a classical dancer performing on stage and TV. I dreamed I was a business owner. I dreamed I drove a convertible. I dreamed a guy loved me, I dreamed I was an author. I didn't know what was in store in my future, but I had visions of "living the dream."

Would it amaze you if I said that all my dreams came true? Some of my plans didn't work out the way I imagined, but when they became reality they turned out better than what I dreamed for myself. My friends graduated, settled into their dream careers, got proposals from their sweethearts, enjoyed the best honeymoon getaways, and had their children. It felt like my life was just passing away like the waves of the ocean, crashing to the shore. My life didn't match the cookie cutter pattern, and I felt something was wrong, not knowing that God's blueprint did not fit my own ideal version of life. Everything came to me sooner or later, just not when -- or exactly how -- I was expecting it.

> *As a child working to help pay the bills, I was constantly daydreaming because that was the only thing I could afford to do.*

The habit of dreaming is like a magnet for dreams to come true. Some call it the "secret" or law of attraction. I know one thing for sure, dreaming and working towards it results in amazing accomplishments.

Physician-Scientist Dr. Sanya Thomas urges adults and children alike, saying, "Never underestimate your capabilities—there is nothing that is beyond your reach if you're willing to pay the price, provided you never compromise on your personal values."

Thomas recommends that everyone do this: "Set clear, concise goals that are time-bound and specific. The best way to ensure you are off to a strong start is to write your goals down. Maintain a journal where you can write about your dreams, and once you have your big goals written down, design a realistic plan with a timeline that would help you achieve your target. And with one step at a time you will be able to set forth on a rewarding journey leading you to success."

Believe in Yourself and Embrace Changes

Someone said, "If you are not afraid, your dream is not big enough." You understand what it means: dreaming big adds discomfort and fear. Maybe that's why some people remain in their safe zone or in their comfort place and choose not to dream.

We all can do some form of great things depending on our mental, physical and emotional abilities. Do you know someone who climbed a corporate ladder without any academic qualifications? Well, I do. I know millionaires who didn't go to college and I know degree holders who doubt their capabilities. It's because the habits of believing in themselves and embracing change are not things that come to many people naturally. They take extra effort and sometimes involve risk.

Doubt holds people back from applying for positions they could carry out. Should I apply for that leadership position? I don't have the qualifications, although I have enough experience to manage the job or role. Remember, nobody is a born leader. It takes courage and a mindset to advance in a position. It also takes learning to meet the requirements. If you are willing to do the work to get where you want, you will somehow achieve your dreams. It's a habit. Some people are better team players than leaders. Their role may seem small or insignificant, however every role is equally important. When we are able to accept our limits and contribute our best, it's enough. A child who has disabilities can also dream big, as long as their achievements are measured against their own potential.

Look for Role Models

Role models can be found at home, school, church, and everywhere we go. For example, when I first moved to the U.S., I found a good role model at a church.

Although I've had many experiences living and working in different countries around the globe, my transition to life in America was the most difficult one. Everything was different here. I had to start all over again; it was as if nothing I ever did before mattered. While trying to figure out this new life in a new country, I visited a church in Dallas, Texas, The Potter's House, where Bishop T.D. Jakes ministers.

Have you attended a talk where you felt the entire message was written just for you? The speaker had sent a spy to gather information about you and worked on answering all the questions that filled your head. I have had this experience many times.

I felt that way when I first heard Bishop T.D. Jakes preaching. I connected with Bishop Jakes and kept searching for his messages on youtube whenever I got a chance. Part of Bishop's sermon on that day was about "Starting From The Corner" to describe the process of moving step-by-step from living isolated and misunderstood to being capable and respected. The message was about being humble to start from the ground up despite our past successes or accomplishments.

"Nobody knows where you come from; nobody cares, nobody understands," he said. "Nobody has been where you lived, nobody has a clue… but you know their culture, you must learn to understand, you must care because you are now here. Start from the corner. It doesn't matter what you've done before, take that job, be a cashier, and start from the corner. Once you have mastered that job, be an administrator, and start from the corner. When you become a manager, start from the corner; when you become the boss, start from the corner, because to master anything at all, you have to be willing to start from the corner."

I felt like he was talking to me because I was so frustrated at how some people spoke or treated me as an immigrant. I had been a manager in other countries. In Malaysia, I owned a car and house, which I purchased with my hard-earned money, but people behaved as if I'd grown up in a tropical jungle wandering the woods with a long spear to hunt, wearing leafy clothes. I would get that idea when they ask questions like, "Do you have Starbucks in Malaysia?" "Do you have Christmas trees?"

Yes, we do! I'd think. We have more than that. How do I explain?

Bam! Just like that, Bishop Jakes' words began repeating in my head all the time, like a mantra. "Start from the corner." "There's no point in being frustrated with people who don't know where I come from. I am here now; Bishop is right; I have to start again because nothing I ever did matters anymore." I told myself.

So, I did just that; wherever I worked, I started from the corner, always willing to learn; as a cashier, in a legal office, and back to school. I decided to pursue a degree since most of my papers were not transferable as they were British-based. I am a boss now, the owner of my store. I have so much to learn and have yet to master the art of being a boss. I am still working from the corner. Bishop Jakes is my spiritual mentor, and it is a gift to have someone who can mentor you without even knowing you in person. I relate to Bishop because his journey in life through poverty to abundance and a mind that overflows with ideas are almost similar to mine. The difference is he has the intellectual ability and wisdom and knows what to do with them while I am still figuring out how to execute my ideas properly for God's glory, feeling unworthy at times to handle significant assignments.

I am sure Bishop Jakes has changed many lives of people around the world through his books and preaching like he did for me. I have read most of his books, which have helped me make life altering decisions. I draw wisdom from the lessons he has learned and experienced; his books are powerful. Although I don't attend his church, I have watched most of his messages online and youtube. Bishop has impacted my life; I hope I can give him a big bear hug to say thank you and tell him that I look up to him as a spiritual father.

Some people find good role models in their families -- dad and mom in some homes, grandparents, single parents, foster parents, or other relatives in other households. It's hard to find good role models at home when mom and dad are both working hard and unable to be fully present to teach and mold a child. My older sister was a remarkable role model for me, one of kindness and love.

I remember one day when we were cruising along at full speed in my sister's car along the usually busy highway in Selangor, Malaysia. The road was surprisingly empty: there were no cars except ours, not even one. My sister suddenly stopped her car, then reversed so fast that it almost gave me a heart attack.

She leaned across me, quickly opened the passenger side door, and yelled, "Pick it up! Pick it up! Quick!!"

I panicked and exclaimed, "What??"

Then I saw what she'd already noticed. She wanted me to pick up an injured black kitten. How had she even spotted it? Well, my sister can spot an injured animal from a distance; that's her superpower. It wasn't my first rescue mission with her.

"Put it on your lap!" she exclaimed. "Pat it, Pam!" She instructed me with disappointment in her voice. Even though I love animals, I was still in shock thinking of the stunt my sister pulled on a typically busy highway. She could have gotten us killed for a kitten.

The bruised kitten looked terrified and pitiful. I was able to calm down eventually and focus on it. It was a tiny, sweet thing. "Do you think Mom will let us keep it?" I asked my sister while patting the little ball of fur. "Maybe just for three days," she said with a sigh. "You know the rules."

My mom was not an animal lover till later when she had our pet dog Rock, a miniature pinscher. Mom's childhood memories of being bitten by a dog haunted her. She never had pets or cared for animals growing up, but she didn't stop us from caring for animals. She had a three-day rule for us: we could bring animals home, clean them up, feed them, and tend to their wounds or injuries, but we had to let them go on the third day.

So, my sister cleaned up the black kitten, applied some medicine to its wounds, gave it some warm milk, and made a comfortable bed using cardboard boxes and old towels. She cared for it, and on the third day, we drove to the alley behind some Chinese restaurants and let the kitten go. I noticed her mumble something to the kitten, probably, "The bins are all yours, kitty, dig in!" or something like that.

My sister's act of kindness didn't end with just one kitten. On another occasion, she rushed home from work on a rainy day, grabbed umbrellas and a large tote bag, seized my hands, and urged me to follow. Since we didn't have a car then, we hopped onto a bus. She stopped at the bus stop where she worked, and although the rain was pouring down, it didn't matter to her. She was focused on rescuing a baby bird that fell out of its nest and was injured. The rain caused the helpless bird to stay on the ground, and my sister feared the water would hurt the bird even more. So, she gently took the birdie and placed it in a large tote bag prepped with comfort. I remember the weird stares we had to ignore as we boarded the bus home, especially when the bird chirped away loudly on the bus. My sister warned me not to make eye contact. It was embarrassing and hilarious because we looked like bird thieves or crooks.

As I have said, my sister had a habit of being kind to animals and people. She loved with all her heart, and that was her only weakness. I once spotted a bunny with a bandaged paw in her apartment. Even when she hardly made enough money as a single mom at one point in life, she would feed families who had less than her. I remember partnering with her to rescue puppies and kittens and joining her in missions to help others.

Acts of kindness like hers come with a cost. The cost includes time, money, and resources such as food and medication. However, the lessons I've learned from her are priceless. Unfortunately, we don't have animal protection services to help in some countries. So we either did something ourselves or left the animals to tend to themselves.

My sister's habits have become part of my habits since we were young. She often says she's so proud of me and cheers me on in whatever I do. But little does she know that she has been a big sister I look up to as a role model in many ways.

The best way to help children who don't have a role model at home is with books and resources that help them succeed. That's even helpful for those who can learn from people at home. Besides my mom, grandma, and aunties, I learned from Oprah Winfrey's TV show, read books and gathered ideas, and received help from others who could pave the way for my dreams. Some kids come out of a bad neighborhood, talk about how unlucky they were and denied resources, and keep blaming it on their circumstances. However, that neighborhood also produces winners who strive to break the generational curse of poverty and bad choices. It's a habit to be controlled by the past, and it's a habit to constantly work towards changing the narrative. It takes more work for some to succeed, but those who come from abusive homes and bad neighborhoods are much stronger and more resilient. These people made it out despite their circumstances, and the stars were the limit.

Our attitude towards life is everything. And we may tend to break down each time we fall. But if we look up to a role model who flourished despite similar experiences, it will help us focus on the goal instead of the problem or circumstances.

Set Goals and Plans-Vision Boards

Vision boards helped me visualize my goals better. I began dreaming big when I was a teenager. I remember watching Oprah Winfrey's TV shows in Malaysia and being inspired by her work as a woman and for women. In one of her shows, she talked about making vision boards. She taught her audience to gather old magazines and cut out pictures or words that described what we liked or dreamed of. For example, if we liked a house, a bicycle or the beach, she suggested that we cut the picture out and create a big collage of pictures and words to inspire us to work towards something we aimed to achieve. It was just a fancier way of goal setting, but let me tell you how powerful vision boards are. I was seventeen when I first started making vision boards. I make one every year and it's pretty amazing to see the results this simple board helped me achieve.

I just read a post on Facebook that said, " The sea is common for all . . . some take pearls, some take fish, some come out just with wet legs! The World is common to all: what we get is what we are looking for." Isn't that profound? Dreams are similar to that. If you dream of a vacation and you want or need a vacation to relieve yourself from a stressful job, then when you do the work of planning, saving up, and booking your flight, being at the beach will become a reality. But first you have to dream or set a goal. When you put your vision on a board, you are constantly reminded of it, and it will easily lead you to achieve your goals.

Make the habit of creating vision boards every year and keep the board in a place where you can see. Add on to it or make a new board the following year. Keep working on your vision till it becomes a reality.

Dream big! When we create fun habits for our children, dreams are no longer too big and difficult to achieve. Instead, they become an activity you can do as a family to achieve goals together. The habit of working together as a family to achieve a dream is also powerful. It takes a lot of coordination, but it is possible.

Put in the Work

My mom picked up a cute accent pillow for me as a Christmas gift one year that said, "Beautiful girl you can do hard things." It was decorated in a bohemian style, with pretty flowers and a splash of bright colors. I found out that the company that carries the pillow has a beautiful collection of unique gifts, and I became a fan in an instant. Only a few stores carried these products, so whenever I needed gifts for my nieces or friends, I would drive to the nearest one—a bakery that also sold these wonderful gifts. I admit: I would get myself a cupcake every time I went there, too. But although the cake was sweet, these gifts were sweeter with meaningful sayings on the bags, mugs, and the famous "giving plates," which are designed to encourage people to share homemade treats with friends.

"You can be everything you want to be and do everything you want to do, but not at the same time."

Beautiful Girl, You Can Do Hard Things

I always imagined owning a boutique carrying artistic, inspiring gifts. I kept dreaming, but never in my wildest dream did I think it was possible. But dreams are God-given. He puts them in our hearts; He understands and knows each and every desire we have, and He also fulfills them in His time. As I was closing one chapter of my life and ending the franchise contract I had, I opened a new business with a creative space and boutique. I Googled the company that sold my favorite bohemian collection to find out if they had a wholesaler deal and I applied for it as soon as I found out that they did. I am so glad I drafted that email and clicked send. I was elated when I received the email that welcomed me as a wholesaler. Now, I sell these pretty, meaningful, bohemian gifts in my own store.

A dream and a wish can become reality when we work towards achieving it. Taking baby steps to achieve a dream is necessary and important because dreaming alone isn't enough. A doctor cannot become a doctor overnight; it takes a dream to fuel his/her drive to take action, which includes years of studying, tons of applications, and a long interview process for medical school, residency and finally a secured job in a clinic or hospital.

Big dreams for people who lack resources could be things like to obtain a bicycle as a form of transportation, to eat three meals a day, or maybe to travel far to visit family. In some rural villages, a big dream might be to have clean water for their daily use. One National Geographic documentary showed young children climbing forty feet down into a well to draw water during a drought. They and their families had a dream of meeting their basic need for water, and they took action to achieve it. But it all starts with the habit of dreaming big! We are destined for greatness, we are the Potter's Child, molded and shaped to be the best version of ourselves.

> *A dream fuels the drive to action.*
>
> *Dreaming alone isn't enough.*
>
> *But it all starts with the habit of dreaming big!*

What if dreams don't come true? What next? How do we overcome disappointment?

I have had many life experiences where dreams seemed far away and unattainable: dropping out of law school, failed relationships, childless for ten years, these are just a few examples. Some dreams came true after years of waiting, for example, having my twins. However, some of my dreams remain just that: mere dreams.

When I presented my business idea to one of my university professors years ago, he asked me to prepare an agenda. I wrote about my goals, which included law school and my business idea for Potter's Child. When he read it, he asked me to pick just one goal. He said, "if you were only able to pick one, which one would you pick?" I said, "Potter's Child?" more like I asked him if that's what he expected me to say. He said, "Great! Yes, that's the right answer. Stephanie, you can be everything you want to be and do everything you want to do, but not at the same time." That was truly an "Aha" moment for me. Recently, Barbara Hemphill told me almost the same thing when she said, "Stephanie, you overflow with ideas and goals, but first, you must learn how to rein your thoughts and execute them one at a time." I was thankful for these mentors who were able to shed clarity to my agenda. It is true that I want to accomplish all my dreams, old and new. The goals clutter my mind and cause disappointment when I fail to achieve them. I set the bar for myself, and it's just a habit. If I get burned out trying to fulfill and accomplish everything I ever wanted to do, all at once, it can be a negative factor and a bad habit which contradicts dreaming big, a positive habit.

When I found out that I was pregnant with my twins, my goals were left on the back burner. I waited ten years to have children, so I had to decide. Business school, law school,

Potter's Child and writing a book had to wait. My priority shifted; bringing healthy babies to the world became my biggest priority. My health was a priority since I was carrying twins and I was at high risk for complications because I was not a young mother.

As a result, law school had to take a back seat once again. Whenever I notice my LSAT (Law School Admission Test) flash cards on my shelf, I sigh with disappointment because my dream of becoming an attorney was one that was always unattainable; something always came up. Why!? I ask myself. It took me back to the time when I followed my mom to the bank to withdraw her last bit of savings so she could enroll me in law school in Malaysia in 1994. I paid for the next two years, but the third year I had to drop out because I couldn't afford the tuition fees anymore. The fees for books, tuition, and exams combined were in sterling pounds since Malaysian law was British-based. That year, our currency was lower than pounds, close to seven times. I remember getting into debt trying to pay off bills and living paycheck to paycheck. Working and paying for my fees at the same time was a challenge, and I couldn't manage on my own anymore as the fees got higher with each passing year. Since it was a private school, I didn't qualify for any grants or loans. Years ago, there were no loans available for studying in Malaysia. Times have changed for the better and almost everyone I know in Malaysia is able to acquire education without struggling the way I did. In Malaysia, we go to law school right after high school, we take an exam called "A levels," and then we pursue law school for five years, unlike in America where we must obtain a bachelor's degree and sit for the LSAT exams, completing them within three years of law school. Again, this dream seemed far from reach. But I remembered how each time I had a plan or a goal, God showed up with something bigger and better. God calls the shots in our lives. Have you heard the song, "Steal My Show"? It's a beautiful song by TobyMac. Part of the song goes like this,

"If you wanna steal my show

I'll sit back and watch you go

If you got something to say

Go on and take it away

Need you to steal my show

Can't wait to watch you go oh oh oh

So take it away"

This song is about letting God steal your show, because when He does, He amplifies it and perfects it to be better than your actual ambition. God's plans for me always exceed what I had in mind. Although I was willing to be single, He blessed me with a loving husband. When I decided to settle for two puppies, He blessed me with twins. And now, He made a way for me to complete this book and pursue my invention to create a board game next. People tell me that the board game era is dying, but I believe that it's time to bring the basics back to our lives which lack socializing opportunities. Maybe someday I will be an attorney. Or maybe not. But I will let God and time decide, because right now, my decision to spend time with my twins is part of God's plans, and it brings me contentment. Our children need us. What we teach and model are more important than just showering them with gifts and education. I count my blessings that I can spend time reading and playing with my children; none of my goals and dreams match the joy that I experience. It was part of the potter's plan.

Whatever you are going through, always be mentally prepared for plan B, C, D . . . Because life will constantly throw curve balls at you and you will have to accept changes, take detours, and pivot—whether you are prepared for it or not. So it is better to be prepared and to prepare your children. The only way you can do this is to trust God. Remember, life here is temporary. If you are a Christian like me, you know that none of these matter: how many awards you have received, your titles, money, fame; you take nothing with you. So, keep that in mind and keep moving forward; you must manage both the highs and lows, and that's what life is all about. If you know ten people, ten stories, you will learn that everyone has a story of facing disappointment at some point in their lives. Nobody walks out without facing rough days and problems. Nobody! When we begin to count our blessings and list all the things we are grateful for, life will keep giving us more reasons to be grateful.

Habits to Practice

One way to practice the habit of dreaming big is to read inspiring biographies of people who have accomplished great things. It's true that some people are more lucky or privileged than others. At the same time, when we read the life stories of successful people, we will learn information and habits that allowed them to achieve their dreams despite their circumstances. Start dreaming for something you always wanted to do, then be ready to do whatever it takes. Make vision boards to motivate and inspire you, and keep them in a place you look at often. These reminders of our dreams are like a magnet to achieving them. It's not a secret! It starts with the habit of dreaming.

Habits to Teach Children

Teach children to dream big. But remember, dreaming alone is not enough. It takes the habit of hard work and discipline to achieve dreams, and achieving them also requires making sacrifices. I believe that the only way we can teach children to dream big is to start first. You cannot teach a child to dream big if you doubt the idea of dreaming big yourself. Inspire children by encouraging them to watch TED Talks given by those who are less fortunate or taking them to the Paralympics to help them see how a person with a physical disability gears up for a competition. Habits form in the mind and the mind is powerful. Our children must remember that life may not be like a fairytale, but some dreams will come true! Make vision boards together with them. And dreams worth attention are not only about big things we can buy, like cars, houses and vacations. Worthwhile dreams could be as simple and immediate as making an "A" in math, buying Nike shoes, learning how to play the guitar or to speak to a friend in their own language. Anything worth doing is worth dreaming. And when we dream, we set possibilities in motion.

Conclusion

<><><><><><><><><><><><><><><><><><><><><><><><><><><><><><><><><><><><>

Our lives are ordained by God. He created us to live a purposeful life, and He is a God who answers prayers. Little things we do daily -- such as taking time to pray, making the bed, cleaning up after ourselves, intentionally building relationships, spending wisely, manners, reading, working hard, playing, dreaming big dreams -- they all become habits that build our character.

Our children are constantly watching our behavior and patterns and are mimicking us. If you don't like what you see in your children, you will have to drop a few of your own bad habits before you attempt to mold them. Everybody has good and bad habits, including me. When a child is growing up, they imitate everyone around them, not knowing the difference between good and bad. As they grow older, they learn the difference and can make choices. Teach children to choose only good habits. It's a struggle to change old ways. Some of us have habits that are hard to break, but if it's inconveniencing others and causing problems in life, why not drop it and make a new habit? New behaviors are easier when they become habits.

> *"Watch your thoughts, they become your words; watch your words, they become your actions; watch your actions, they become your habits; watch your habits, they become your character; watch your character, it becomes your destiny."*
>
> **- Anonymous**

Endnotes

<<<<<<<<<<<<<<<<<<<<<<<<<<<<<<<<<<<<<<<<<<<<<<<<<<<<<<<<<<<

Chapter 1 The Power of Prayer

[1]You'll find Hagar in Genesis 21, Leah in Genesis 29, and Ruth has an entire book of the Bible about her, the book of Ruth.

[2]In Joshua 1:1-9 (ESV), God tells the young man Joshua that he will lead the nation of Israel into the long promised territory. "Be strong and courageous," God repeats. "Be strong and very courageous … Do not be frightened and do not be dismayed, for the Lord your God is with you wherever you go."

Chapter 2: Make Your Bed

[3]Admiral William H. McRaven, University of Texas at Austin 2014 Commencement Address. May 19, 2014.

https://www.youtube.com/watch?v=pxBQLFLei70

[4]SARAH AGUIRRE, A List of Age-Appropriate Chores for Kids 2 to 18. Updated on June 21, 2022.

https://www.thespruce.com/age-appropriate-chore-charts-1900357

[5]William H. McRaven. Make Your Bed: Little Things that Can Change Your Life and Maybe the World. Grand Central Publishing, 2017. https://www.amazon.com/Make-Your-Bed-Little-Things/dp/1455570249

Chapter 3 Clean Up, Wash Up

[6]Water, Sanitation, and Environmentally Related Hygiene (WASH). Page last reviewed: June 15, 2022.

https://www.cdc.gov/hygiene/fast-facts.html

Chapter 4 Please, Thank you, I am Sorry, Excuse Me

[7]Julian Baggini, How to live, love (and text) in the 21st century. November 25, 2004.

https://www.theguardian.com/theguardian/2004/nov/25/features11.g2

[8]DanaHolmes, MANNERS MONDAY: EXCUSE ME?.

https://metromomclub.com/manners-monday-excuse-me/

Chapter 5 Money Matters

[9]Money Ruining Marriages in America: A Ramsey Solutions study

FEBRUARY 6, 2018

https://www.ramseysolutions.com/company/newsroom/releases/money-ruining-marriages-in-america

[10]The Knot Unveils 2010 Real Weddings Survey Results. March 02, 2011

https://www.businesswire.com/news/home/20110302005388/en/The-Knot-Unveils-2010-Real-Weddings-Survey-Results

[11]When Christians give ten percent to the church, they call it tithing. Tithe is a word that means "tenth."

[12]Easy Ways To Teach Kids About Taxes. (2014, August 21). Retrieved October 27, 2020.

https://www.optimataxrelief.com/3-easy-ways-teach-kids-taxes/

[13]Explaining Taxes to Kids Lesson Plan. (2020). Retrieved October 27, 2020.

https://www.usa.gov/taxes-lesson-plan

Chapter 6 Work Hard, Play Harder

[14] Despain, M., Teaching Children Hard Work and Determination. Retrieved October 16, 2020.

https://kidsvillage.com/teaching-values-hard-work-and-determination/

[15]Lisa Quast, Why Grit Is More Important Than IQ When You're Trying To Become Successful. Mar 6, 2017.

https://www.forbes.com/sites/lisaquast/2017/03/06/why-grit-is-more-important-than-iq-when-youre-trying-to-become-successful/?sh=4bc1524f7e45

[16]Steinhoff, A. (2016, August 23). Why Winning and Losing Is Important for Children. Retrieved October 23, 2020.

https://novakdjokovicfoundation.org/winning-losing-important-children

[17]Steinhoff, A. (2016, August 23). Why Winning and Losing Is Important for Children. Retrieved October 23, 2020.

https://novakdjokovicfoundation.org/winning-losing-important-children/

[18]Steinhoff, A. (2016, August 23). Why Winning and Losing Is Important for Children. Retrieved October 23, 2020.

https://novakdjokovicfoundation.org/winning-losing-important-children/

[19]The Power of Play - How Fun and Games Help Children Thrive. (2019, November 25). Retrieved October 23, 2020.

https://www.healthychildren.org/English/ages-stages/toddler/fitness/Pages/Caution-Children-at-Play.aspx

[20]The Power of Play - How Fun and Games Help Children Thrive. (2019, November 25). Retrieved October 23, 2020.

https://www.healthychildren.org/English/ages-stages/toddler/fitness/Pages/Caution-Children-at-Play.aspx

[21]Dr. Amanda Gummer, 14 REASONS TO PLAY AT EVERY AGE - The Benefits of Intergenerational Play - for Children, Parents & Grandparents.

https://thegeniusofplay.org/genius/expert-advice/articles/14-reasons-to-play-at-every-age.aspx#.Y1gRbXZByUl

Chapter 7 Building Relationships

[22]The concept of a relationship "trust bank" may originate with Stephen Covey. It appears in his 1997 book, The 7 Habits of Highly Effective Families: Creating a Nurturing Family in a Turbulent World.

[23]Brian A. "Drew" Chalker, Reason, Season and a Lifetime.

https://sarazarrella.com/2010/12/reason-season-and-a-lifetime-poem/

[24]Eggerich, Emerson. *Love and Respect*: The Love She Most Desires; The Respect He Desperately Needs. Thomas Nelson, 2004

[25]Leo, P. (1989). Teaching Children Respect. Retrieved October 16, 2020.

https://www.naturalchild.org/articles/pam_leo/respect.html

Chapter 8 Time Management

[26] Shalini Paruthi, MD*, Lee J. Brooks, MD, Carolyn D'Ambrosio, MD, Wendy A. Hall, PhD, RN, Suresh Kotagal, MD, Robin M. Lloyd, MD, Beth A. Malow, MD, MS, Kiran Maski, MD, Cynthia Nichols, PhD, Stuart F. Quan, MD, Carol L. Rosen, MD, Matthew M. Troester, DO, Merrill S. Wise, MD, Recommended Amount of Sleep for Pediatric Populations: A Consensus Statement of the American Academy of Sleep Medicine Shalini Paruthi, Published OnlineJune 15, 2016.

https://jcsm.aasm.org/doi/10.5664/jcsm.5866

Published Online:June 15, 2016 by:397

Chapter 9 Read and Learn

[27] John Gray (1992). *Men Are from Mars, Women Are from Venus.*

A portion of the proceeds
of this book benefit Equest

Available in
Paperback, Hardback,
eBook, and Audiobook
EVERYWHERE books
are sold.

More from
Stephanie Mathews

potterschild.com

Made in the USA
Middletown, DE
26 November 2022

15780070R00177